Mask-Making
With Pantomime
and Stories
From American History

Other Books by Laura Ross

HOLIDAY PUPPETS
FINGER PUPPETS: Easy to Make, Fun to Use
PUPPET SHOWS: Using Poems and Stories
HAND PUPPETS: How to Make and Use Them

Mask-Making With Pantomime and Stories From American History

Laura Ross

Drawings by Frank Ross, Jr.
Constructed mask photos by George Haddad

Lothrop, Lee & Shepard Company
A Division of WILLIAM MORROW & COMPANY, INC.
NEW YORK

Library of Congress Cataloging in Publication Data
Ross, Laura.
  Mask-making with pantomime and stories from American history.

  SUMMARY: Instructions for making masks and using them with pantomime in dramatizations of four popular stories from American history.
    1. Masks—Juvenile literature. 2. United States—History—Drama. [1. Masks.
2. Pantomine. 3. United States—History—Drama] I. Ross, Frank Xavier (date)
II. Title.
TT898.R67   792.3'026   75-11960
ISBN 0-688-41721-3
ISBN 0-688-51721-8

U. S. 1917852

For all children who love to masquerade

Contents

Foreword

Masks were used by the ancient Greeks and Romans in pantomime on the dramatic stage and mask-making as an art is having a revival in modern times. Many dramatic incidents in American history lend themselves to pantomime.

Indians, Eskimos, blacks, and whites—women and men—have played important parts in the story of our nation. It is my intention to show how masks can be made and used with pantomime to dramatize stories of individuals who have made important contributions in the growth of America.

The stories have been included primarily to supplement mask-making. They have been rewritten to combine pantomime with spoken dialogue, and also to make use of a narrator offstage. I have tried to combine the human element with the historical incident, and to condense and telescope events to keep the action moving rapidly on the stage. The stories included are for those who do not wish to write their own. But it would be fun to write some yourself, so feel free to do so.

The techniques for making the different masks are interchangeable. For example, directions for making the papier-mâché mask for the story of the discovery of the North Pole can be used to make a mask for any of the other stories. We will make only one mask for each story. Masks for the other characters in each of the stories may be made similarly or you may wish to create your own.

Most of the techniques of mask-making are shown with diagrams but since the papier-mâché mask utilizes a step-by-step process of clay modeling, I have used a series of photos to show the progression of the work.

This book is intended for beginners in mask and mime. The stories and mask-making progress from the simple to the more difficult and hopefully will lead the reader to original creations.

Mask-Making
With Pantomime
and Stories
From American History

*Ceremonial wooden mask from the Nunivak tribe
of Eskimos, Alaska. It is colored dark red and black.
Rings are tied together with sinew.
Ornaments of wood and feathers are attached.*
COURTESY UNIVERSITY OF ALASKA MUSEUM

History of the Mask

Masks were used by primitive people as a passport into the imaginative world. They sought to explain nature in terms of spirits dwelling within the clouds, the wind, the trees, and so on. Primitive men and women believed that these spirits had the power to work good or evil in their behalf and masks were the means by which they attempted to communicate with and dominate these powerful spirits. When they put on their masks they felt a god-like power and strength. They sought the intervention of the spirits in such matters of daily life as births, weddings, or sickness. Through offerings and prayers expressed in masked ceremonial mime and dance, they attempted to dominate and master these mysterious spirits and thereby control the fall of rain, the success of the hunt, or the bounty of the harvest.

This belief in the supernatural power of the mask was held by primitive people in all parts of the world.

In Africa, masks were created by the artists of the tribes and were always worn in tribal religious rites. These masks did not represent the natural face, but greatly exaggerated the facial features to give intensity of expression. The masks were

13

strange in appearance, but not terrifying. They were made of wood, copper, and ivory. When the mask was worn by the religious person, he felt no longer like himself, but more like the spirit of the god whose help he was seeking.

The ancient Egyptians used masks in their sacrificial ceremonies. Artifacts and paintings on the walls of tombs unearthed by archaeologists show scenes of sacrifices with priests wearing masks. One scene in particular depicts a human sacrifice to the great Egyptian god Osiris. The chief priest is shown wearing a mask of a jackal. His assistants are wearing masks of the hare and the hawk.

Other ancient paintings show Egyptian kings wearing masks representing the lion and the bull. They wore these facial adornments to impress their subjects with their mighty royal power.

Mummies, especially those of dead kings, were masked before burial. The masks were frequently adorned with precious stones and some even made of pure gold.

Masks made by the primitive peoples in North America were quite different. The Eskimo in Alaska believed that every living creature had a double existence and could change at will into the form of a human being or an animal. When an animal wished to become human, it simply raised its foreleg or wing and pushed up its muzzle or beak as if it were a mask and instantly became human in appearance. To represent this duality, Eskimo masks were carved out of wood and ingeniously made as double faces—one of an animal and the other of a man. These were put together with the help of wooden pegs in such a way that at certain stages in a festive ceremony, the outer mask of the animal face could be lifted up and thrown to the back of the head, exposing the mask of a man.

The Eskimos also believed that after death their ancestors watched over them in the forms of animals such as the wolf,

Witch doctor's cowrie shell mask,
Bushongo tribe, Belgian Congo, Africa.
COURTESY UNIVERSITY OF PENNSYLVANIA MUSEUM

Eskimo Shaman's wooden mask, from northern Alaska.
COURTESY UNIVERSITY OF PENNSYLVANIA MUSEUM

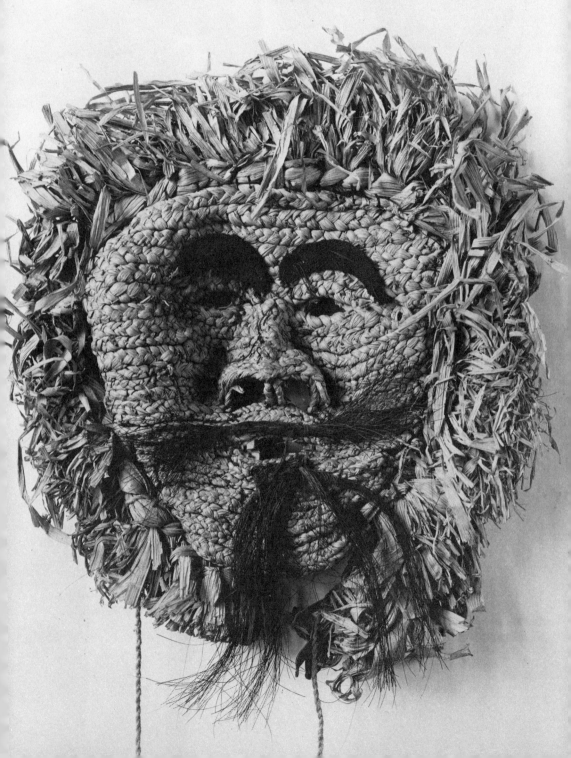

*Wooden mechanical mask representing an eagle
from the Indians of British Columbia.*
COURTESY MUSEUM OF THE AMERICAN INDIAN, HEYE FOUNDATION

beaver, or various birds. They made masks of these creatures and believed that the spirits of the creatures entered into their bodies when they wore the masks. They felt that they acquired supernatural powers which allowed them to call on their ancestors for aid, to assure the tribe of a successful hunt or good health.

Indians in the northwestern part of the United States used masks in an annual ceremony that mourned the dead. Men prepared themselves to represent the ghosts of their departed. They painted masks and decorated them with feathers and grasses. With these as a disguise, they danced and sang in the village or rushed about through the woods bearing flaming torches. The mask wearers were looked upon by those watching as departed friends and relatives.

18

The Indians of the southwestern United States, the Hopi and Zuni among others, also used masks to worship their departed ancestors. They believed that their dead became supernatural spirits continually passing over the plains and gathering water in vases and gourds from the great rivers.

During critical periods of drought Indians donned their sacred masks and performed the rain dance. If the departed ancestors responded, they sprinkled precious water from their vases and gourds on the parched land below. The Indians often felt that the spirits could not be seen by them because the spirits wore cloud masks.

Other American Indian tribes used a variation of the mask for their festivities and solemn ceremonies. They painted their faces with elaborate designs in red, yellow, green and blue. The designs most commonly used represented the sun, moon, stars, crosses, and birds.

In Brazil, the primitive Indians made and wore masks representing animals, birds, and insects. Wearers of these masks believed they acquired magical powers by imitating the movements of such creatures as the jaguar, toad, parrot, spider, vulture, and beetle.

Masks originated in Asia just as they did in Africa and America, as a result of man's superstitions. In India, China, Japan, and throughout the Orient, they have been used for centuries in religious ceremonies. Gradually they were introduced into court and social functions such as weddings and birthdays. Eventually animal masks were used in street festivals to entertain the common people.

The Orientals created masks of great intricacy, sophistication, and often of considerable beauty. They were very good at recognizing and expressing emotions such as anger, humor, and tranquility in their masks.

Masks were a popular device of the priests in China to

Ceremonial mask, Singalese people, Ceylon.
COURTESY UNIVERSITY OF PENNSYLVANIA MUSEUM

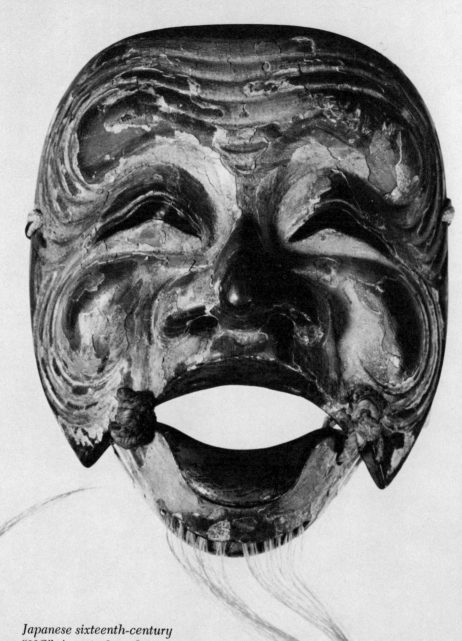

*Japanese sixteenth-century
"NO" theatrical mask
of carved wood with gesso finish.
Old man's smiling face is deeply wrinkled;
lower jaw is hinged.*
COURTESY ROYAL ONTARIO MUSEUM

Theatrical character masks from Japan.
COURTESY UNIVERSITY OF PENNSYLVANIA MUSEUM

pantomime stories that told of the rewards of living a good life, and the punishments of living a bad one. The masks had terrifying as well as amusing features. They were rarely beautiful. The masks were worn by costumed priests who enacted their moralistic stories in pantomime on a stage erected in temple courtyards.

In Siam, Burma, Java, and Ceylon, masks were widely employed in secular activities. They were used in theatrical plays and were favorite devices of strolling street entertainers.

Probably the most beautiful masks in the world are the religious or *No* masks of Japan. These are used in the "NO" plays, the classical drama of the Japanese aristocracy. These ancient stories of the gods and their victories over demons have been performed for over 600 years on simple outdoor stages.

Masks were widely used in ancient Greece and Rome, mainly for the drama and occasions of public festivals. It is from these countries that we have inherited the mask as an artistic device for the dramatic stage.

Because ancient Greek dramas were performed in large outdoor amphitheaters, the mask was created and used to better convey the emotions of the characters being portrayed by the performers. Exaggerated expressions on masks enabled actors to be seen more clearly by the audience in the farthest reaches of the amphitheater.

Masks also helped to carry the voices of the performers. They were made with large opened lips, like the curved edges of a clamshell, so that an actor's voice could be heard a great distance from the stage. Sometimes a brass trumpet was attached to the mask to amplify the voice of an actor even more.

By quickly changing different kinds of masks Greek stage performers were able to play a variety of characters, male and female. They could portray youth, middle age, and old age during a single performance.

The ancient Romans used the mask in drama much the same way as the Greeks, and historians tell us that they also employed masks for certain superstitious customs. For example, masks of particular supernatural deities were hung on trees at planting time to insure a successful crop. Also, Roman nobles wore masks at the funerals of departed family members.

With the end of the ancient Roman civilization, masks fell into disuse. Indeed, early Christians frowned upon the use of the mask as a pagan practice. In later times, however, there was a revival of masks, especially throughout the lands of

northern Europe. Masks were used by the peoples of many countries in rites celebrating the start of a new year and the coming of spring.

As the popularity of masks again increased, they gradually made their way into church activities, and were used in the performance of religious stories. In the course of time these stories tended to become more non-religious than religious and in 1207 the Pope prohibited the use of masks in the Church.

Despite the Pope's ban, the use of masks continued to increase in popularity, especially in the enacting of Biblical plays at Christmastime. These plays were performed outside the Church and were called "miracle" or "morality" plays.

From the 14th to the 17th centuries, the mask enjoyed a golden revival in Italy. It was widely employed by troupes of actors touring the towns and cities of their country. They would quickly set up their stage in the marketplaces and proceed to entrance their audiences with the humorous and roguish antics of the characters of the *Commedia dell'arte*. The performers wore particular types of masks to portray particular characters and these masks became recognized as character types in theatrical circles far and wide. There was Harlequin, a clown and acrobat who wore a black, cat-like, half mask; Pulcinella, a humpback with a crooked nose; Pantalone, a wealthy merchant who was a miser and buffoon; and the Doctor, a pompous and devious individual.

There were several other Commedia characters as well and eventually the renown of the troupe traveled beyond the boundaries of Italy into other lands and languages. In the 18th century the comedy theater in France, also using masks, portrayed the antics of the characters of the Commedia, changing Italian names to French.

Although masks in North and South America existed in primitive times, the origin of the popular mask dates its arrival in America with migration from Europe. However, it experienced little importance other than being a plaything for children. Commonly referred to as a "false face" it was used by children for antics at Thanksgiving and Halloween.

Adults came to use the mask at certain social functions such as at masked balls. Perhaps the best known adult use of the mask occurs during Mardi Gras time in New Orleans. In the course of this event, large numbers of the City's inhabitants and out-of-town visitors don colorful costumes and masks for one final riotous, explosion of fun—in public and private—before the start of Lent and its period of austere living.

The Chinese also brought the traditional use of the mask with them to the United States. In their communities throughout this country, the Chinese New Year is ushered in with joyous street festivities. Highlight of the gaiety is a giant, colorful dragon writhing its way along the parade route. One man manipulates the head, or mask, from the interior by holding it over his head and shoulders and walking with it. Other men occupy the hind portions of the dragon, and twist and turn it in a serpentine manner to the accompaniment of a beating drum.

In more recent years there has been a trend toward the serious use of masks in the American theater. They are becoming increasingly evident in television shows, and particularly in live puppetry. Sesame Street, a very fine and popular childrens' program uses extremely imaginative head masks.

Bil Baird, an outstanding American puppeteer, and his son Peter, have designed and created exceptionally beautiful and artistic masks for use in their musical production of *Pinocchio*. Live puppeteers wearing masks perform along with the marionettes for an imaginative and creative work of art. Performances of this outstanding puppet show are put on regularly at the Bil Baird Theater in New York City.

Peter Baird as Alex the Barker,
wearing a half mask made of celastic,
in the musical marionette production of Pinocchio.
COURTESY NAT MESSIK

People of the theater search constantly for new ways to heighten the dramatic interest of plays. They seek to capture more fully the hearts and minds of their audiences. More and more they are making and using masks to achieve this goal. Dramatists and audiences are bound to be intrigued by the revival and use of this old, but new art form.

28

History of Pantomiming

Pantomime is an ancient dramatic art which conveys an idea or story without speech, through movement of the body. A mime is an actor who performs or illustrates the story. If desired, a narrator can be used to tell the story while the actor concentrates on the movements required to dramatize it. Pantomiming usually refers to the entire dramatic performance. Miming refers to the movements of the performer.

Thousands of years ago stories were recited, sung, and dramatized. Primitive people communicated with expressive gestures in the shadows of their caves. It is not difficult to imagine prehistoric man returning to his shelter after a day's hunt and relating to friends the happenings of the day by means of gestures and sounds. No doubt he told them about how bravely he pursued his hunt or if he had been prevented from success by the evil spirits. Later, when primitive people became more imaginative, they performed pantomime dances or invocations to influence the gods for success in the hunt. In more recent times, the Zuni Indians of the American Southwest dramatized stories in the form of pantomime to celebrate an event and also to influence the gods to bring rain for their crops.

The Hopi Indians are famous for their Serpent Dance which tells the story of their survival from a flood. The Aleutian Indians still pantomime a story of a hunter who fells a beautiful bird which turns into a lovely maiden.

In the Far East—Bali and Siam, for example—ancient pantomiming became a popular means for enacting legends and myths. The mimes performed stories of good and evil spirits who compete for the control of human beings, and the rewards after death for living a good life.

A more sophisticated form of ancient pantomiming took place during the golden age of Greece. Stories of the nature of human life were dramatized on stages of large outdoor theaters, some of which could seat as many as 30,000 people.

Greek pantomimists were highly skilled professionals. They wore large masks in order to be seen from the farthest reaches of an amphitheater and relied on gestures, as much as upon words, to communicate with their audiences. These gestures became a language of the theater that was easily understood by audiences. Actors learned how to use their hands to express the meanings of a story. Pantomiming, combined with the wearing of masks, permitted Greek actors to assume different roles in a single performance—young, middle-aged, old—male or female.

Greek theatrical pantomiming developed along with Greek drama and the two became inseparable. This was due largely to the tradition of the theater which decreed that a Greek tragedy could not have more than three speaking parts. Therefore, all other characters had to be portrayed in pantomime. It is believed that most of the pantomiming in Greek dramas was performed by a choral group which mimed in rhythm while the principal characters stood still and recited their lines.

Whereas the Greeks used pantomime as an accompaniment to spoken words, the Romans pantomimed without words. Some authorities on pantomiming consider the Roman style to be the purest form of the art. There is an old theatrical legend that tells how Roman pantomime came into existence.

It seems there was a great Greek actor who came to Rome to perform in a drama. In the course of the play, he suddenly lost his voice. Equal to the emergency, the actor continued his performance by pantomiming. The audience loved what the actor did and acting without words became a popular device of the Roman theater.

The Roman theater also made use of masks for many stage productions. Roman dramatic productions, like those of the Greeks, were given in large outdoor theaters where actors needed masks to project character moods. Since Roman actors preferred wordless pantomiming, their masks were different from those of the Greeks and were made with closed mouths.

During the Middle Ages, the Church made common use of the techniques of the theater, including pantomiming, to teach religious beliefs to the people. On Holy Days, such as Christmas, Good Friday, and Easter, priests would pantomime incidents appropriate to the occasion. Out of these simple performances came the mystery, miracle, and morality plays in which pantomiming played a major part.

In addition to these sacred plays there were many stage performances given all over Europe by the townspeople and peasants. They would act, mostly in pantomime, on makeshift stages erected in marketplaces, at country fairs, and in the great halls of the castles.

In Italy during the 16th and 17th centuries, the performers

of the Commedia dell'arte, which was discussed in the previous chapter, were highly skilled in the arts of pantomime and improvisation. They traveled through the towns and cities of Italy and eventually to Spain, France, and finally to England, where their coarse humor was enjoyed by all.

Pantomime for the theater came to the United States around the 18th century. Clowns in traveling circuses were probably the first to introduce this art form to American audiences. Their broadly humorous antics were carried out almost entirely through pantomime. Audiences warmly appreciated the silent storytellers, and still do.

Pantomiming became a highly essential tool in the enormous popularity of the silent motion picture. Actors and actresses of the silent films had to portray the feelings of the characters of the stories they told through facial expressions and gestures of the arms and hands. They carried the art of pantomime to new heights of attainment. The coming of sound motion pictures, however, threw the silent films and their art of pantomiming into the discard almost overnight.

In recent years there has been a serious revival of pantomiming in the United States and Europe, particularly in television entertainment. A number of TV performers, both in this country and abroad—Sid Caesar, Red Skelton, and Marcel Marceau among others—have delighted millions of viewers with pantomime. This interest in pantomime is also being stimulated by professional entertainment groups in cities and towns throughout the United States. At school and social functions of all sorts, they are delighting audiences with this ancient art form. All these developments are enormously encouraging for the future of pantomime.

Materials for Use in Mask-Making

Masks can be made from many materials. Some you may consider using (other than those which are suggested for the projects in this book) are the following:

1. Paper plates make quick, easy masks. Draw and cut facial features with felt marking pens, attach a rod to one side with tape and presto, you have a mask. They can also be tied to the face with string.

2. Strong paper such as brown paper bags from the supermarket can also be used. Cut open and glue several layers tightly together. After the mask has been shaped and cut, cover it inside and out with waterproof varnish for durability.

3. Aluminum foil can be molded over a face with your fingers.

4. Aluminum TV dinner trays can make fascinating masks. Cut pieces to cover cheekbones, forehead, etc. Staple the pieces together. Color with inks or colored felt marking pens. To prevent any scratching from the staples on the inner side of the mask, cover the inner side with masking tape.

5. Small cowrie seashells and beads have been used by the Bakuba tribe of the Congo in mask-making and can be glued on a rigid construction paper base cut to fit over your face (similar to the Harriet Tubman mask on page 80).

33

6. Large seeds such as lentil and split peas can also be glued over a rigid construction paper base.

7. Cornhusks or braided raffia can be shaped and glued together to form an oval or glued over a rigid construction paper base.

8. Construction paper glued with colored paper or even pieces of burlap over it, cut and shaped into large planes, makes an interesting mask. This is accomplished by drawing a full-scale pattern for your mask on paper. Divide and define the drawing into large planes such as the forehead, cheeks, and chin. Cut and hinge the pieces together with glued strips of linen, strong paper, or masking tape on the outside and inside. Apply varnish on the outer and inner side of the mask. When dry, finish it off with oil colors. This mask would be challenging to an advanced student familiar with facial anatomy.

9. Plastic gallon bottles can be cut and made into basic masks.

10. Ends of pinecones, small bottle tops, sections of egg cartons, drinking straws, beads, buttons, corrugated cardboard, feathers, pipe cleaners, brush bristles, macaroni etc. can be used for facial features. Pieces of wood shavings and yarn are useful for hair and beard. Cotton soaked in glue and modeled onto wires to the desired shape and size can be used for a moustache. In fact almost any material on hand can be used with a little imagination.

11. For gluing, do not use ordinary glue. If you do, it may dry up, become brittle, and eventually crack. Library paste and paste made with flour and water are usable with paper. For best results with heavier materials use wallpaper paste, which can be purchased inexpensively in small amounts from the hardware store.

12. Colored or black felt pens, crayons, or oil paints can be used to draw features or color a mask.

Some Things to Consider in Mask-Making

1. We shall not attempt to make a portrait mask, that is, one identical in appearance to the character. This is difficult for the beginner. Instead, we will try to make a character mask which exaggerates and emphasizes distinctive features of the individual. For example, the Pocahontas mask will be identified by long, black, braided hair and a feather or two.

2. There are four different types of masks to choose from to make your own: A) A small mask which covers only the front part of the face. This is tied around the head by means of a string attached on both sides of the mask (see the drawing for the Harriet Tubman mask on page 80). B) A half mask which does not cover the entire face but ends at the tip of the nose. This is the type of mask that was worn by the Commedia dell'arte players. It exposes the mouth, jaw, and chin of the wearer, allowing complete freedom to speak naturally. The half mask can be seen in the photo of Peter Baird as the Barker in Pinocchio (see page 28). The buckram mask for the story of the Boston Tea Party (page 65) is also a half mask. C) A medium-size mask which covers the face and the top of the head. This type of mask is held against the face

35

by a top portion which rests over the head (see the drawing for the cage mask on page 40). D) A head mask which covers the head entirely and rests on the shoulders (see the drawing for the Pocahontas mask on page 53).

3. Before making the mask of a particular character, consult books, magazines, etc. to see what he or she looked like. Study the features to help in your interpretation of the character.

4. Draw a few simple pencil sketches of your character's face. Accent and experiment with features particularly characteristic of the person. These features may include high or shallow cheekbones, a large or flat nose, a round or long face, etc.

5. Decide what features of the character you will emphasize for distance recognition. Decide what material or technique will lend itself best for making a particular mask.

6. Sometimes the addition of color is just as important as the shape of the mask. For example, a mop of red hair or shoulder length black hair can be more noticeable than a long nose or protruding chin.

7. Eyeholes are made for seeing. Therefore, cut out eye openings that are large enough. If a mask has painted or constructed eyes, a fixed stare will result. Masks with a fixed stare are usually meant to frighten or amuse. They are made with oddly-shaped eyes. The wearer of such a mask must prolong his stare in one direction, then swiftly move his head in another direction.

8. Nose holes are made for breathing. If you wish, you can simply make an opening on the mask large enough for your nose to fit through. You can also cut the nose of the mask to fit over your own, leaving the bottom of the hole open for breathing.

9. A large mask will give the impression of a small body. A small mask will give the impression of a large body.

10. A mask has to be slightly larger than the wearer's face

or else it will be uncomfortable to wear. However, a mask too large will be out of proportion with the body. A mask of average size (not made to fit specific dimensions) can be worn by a number of people.

11. The main measurements for a custom-made full mask (to fit the face of a specific person) are: the length from the top of the forehead under the hairline to a little below the chin, and the width across the face from ear to ear. Measure also the length from the bridge of the nose to the chin and the width from eye to eye. Measure the width of each eye from corner to corner to be sure of a large enough opening. Measure the width of the bottom of the nose for the same reason.

12. To make your mask look right from all sides when finished, view it from all angles while working on it—from above, from the sides and from below. In this manner you can decide if adjustments need to be made, such as a larger nose, eyes, or mouth.

13. If a mask is too large or the eye level is wrong, you can correct the fault by stuffing a handkerchief between the top of the mask and the head.

14. To attach a small mask to your head, place it over your face so that it fits comfortably. With a pencil, lightly mark the places at either side of the temples. Remove the mask from your face and with a sharp pointed tool (the point of a scissors will do) make a hole large enough to fit a strong rubber band through. To reinforce the hole, attach a piece of masking tape on the inner side of the mask, and redefine the opening. Insert one end of the rubber band through the hole (see sketch). This will form a loop. Insert the other end of the same rubber band through the loop and pull firmly. This will attach the rubber band to the mask. Tie one end of a piece of strong string through the free end of the rubber band. The string must be shorter than the distance around the back

37

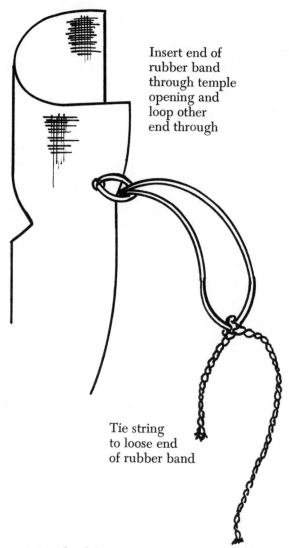

Insert end of
rubber band
through temple
opening and
loop other
end through

Tie string
to loose end
of rubber band

A Method for Attaching Mask to Face

of the head. Do the same with the other side, using another
rubber band and the other end of the same piece of string.
The elasticity of the rubber bands will enable you to fit the
mask over your face and stretch the elastic with the attached
string over the back of the head to hold.

38

15. An informal mask may be attached to a thin stick or dowel and held against the face (see sketch). This will limit the movement in miming, but can be used for large crowd scenes.

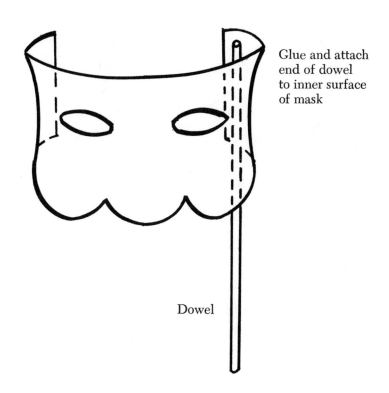

Glue and attach
end of dowel
to inner surface
of mask

Dowel

Half Mask With Dowel Attachment

16. Another way to attach a mask to the face is to construct a cage with firm construction paper cut into strips ½ inch wide and glued or stapled to the inner edge of the mask. First attach a strip to the edge behind the mask from ear to ear. Then attach two more strips at the back of the mask from the

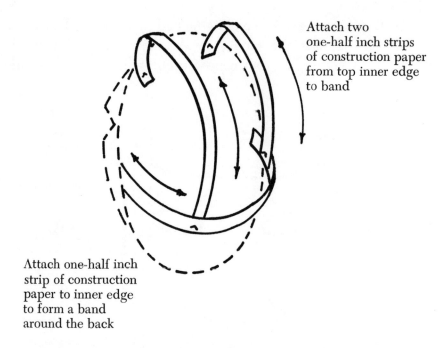

Attach two
one-half inch strips
of construction paper
from top inner edge
to band

Attach one-half inch
strip of construction
paper to inner edge
to form a band
around the back

Back View of Cage Construction on Medium Size Mask

top to the band around it. This forms a sort of cage which will
enable you to slip the mask over your head and allow for
decorating with hair or a headdress (see sketch).

Some Things to Consider in Pantomiming

1. Miming is best learned through observation, practice, exercises, application, and performance before a live audience.
2. Miming is a physical activity and control of your body muscles is important. Sports such as tennis and basketball can be very useful in developing these muscles. Even brisk walks and running can be helpful.
3. Concentration on what your body muscles are doing is most important to controlling your actions. Practice some simple activities and be very much aware of what you are doing, step-by-step, at all times. For example, what do you do when you pull down on a rope? Both hands grasp the rope, one above the other. Both feet are planted firmly on the floor. Your arms pull down, the elbows bending downward. Your knees bend and your body assumes a sitting position. Then up go the knees and legs and the body is straightened as the elbows unbend and arms are lifted.
4. Miming also requires practice in body movements. Practice before a mirror is helpful, but do not limit seeing yourself to this method of observation. Ask a friend to watch you and tell you what it is you are trying to say in silent gestures. Turn it into a charade.

5. Techniques of miming can be built up by observing how other people move or act under all situations. How they use their feet, legs, hands, arms, heads; how they walk, run, turn around; how they perform simple everyday chores such as lifting, pulling, eating, sewing, ironing, etc.

6. When lines are read by an offstage narrator, the movements of the performer should exactly match the timing of the spoken words. To be able to do this, the performer must know the story so well that he will always be aware of the sequence of the action. Therefore, in changing movement or position, think ahead. For example, if three steps are to be taken forward, followed by a turn around, you must anticipate, while taking the third step, that the next action will be to turn around.

7. Most of all, move only on important words. Do not spend too much time on actions that are not important, and skim through those that are. If necessary, repeat the important actions while the narrator pauses. For example, in the Harriet Tubman story, the runaway slaves are in constant fear that they will be caught. When the narrator relates this, the slaves can show their fear by hiding behind the shrubbery and peeking out repeatedly while the narrator pauses.

8. In pantomiming, remember that sometimes there are imaginary objects before you, as for example, a door. You cannot see it but you know it is there. Therefore, know that when knocking you must stop your hand at a certain distance, pretending that the door really is there.

9. Do not be rigid in your movements. Relax and be natural. Be truthful with your actions. For instance, in lifting a heavy box of tea as in the Boston Tea Party story, the weight of the box should be imagined, felt, and shown with a strenuous movement of your arms and shoulders. Exaggerate your actions to communicate very clearly what you wish to say to your audience.

10. Certain pantomime gestures are standard. For example, a

finger over the lips means silence. The hand to the forehead expresses sorrow. A shake of the head and a wave of the hand may mean "no." Moving your index finger back and forth, away and toward you, can be a beckoning gesture.

11. Remember, when coordinating mime with a story that mime deals with the present, never the past or future. If necessary, let the narrator read those details before the story starts, or while it is in progress.

12. In miming, as in all works of art, there is no exact duplication to express an idea. Therefore, performances are re-created each time they are mimed.

13. Mime is a very individual performance. Learn what you can by observation, then invent what appeals to you. Once you have acquired experience at it, you can enlarge, elaborate, and create your own forms of mime to suit a particular story. Bring something of yourself to miming, whether it be your special technique of actions or emotions, and you will have your very own style of performance.

Some Things to Consider in Wearing the Mask With Pantomime

1. When a mask is worn by a performer, his or her personality becomes subordinate to that of the character which the mask represents. He or she also assumes the personality of that character and changes his or her body movements accordingly and acts out emotions awakened by the wearing of the mask.

2. The position of the head, neck, and shoulders, as well as movements of the entire body are used to convey a particular mood. For example; the head tilted up gives the impression of courage, aggressiveness, or defiance; the head tilted down signifies sorrow, worry, gloom, or timidity.

3. A mask viewed from different angles will come alive more readily than if viewed only from the front. The rigid features of the mask, when seen from different angles—with the head tilted up or down, or slanted sideways to left or right—will give the illusion of different emotions or feelings. Try as much as posible to conceal the back of the head.

4. Do not stand stiff and motionless when you wear a mask. Life is added by a slight movement of the head, by the feet shifting from one to the other, and the arms and hands gesticulating.

5. Mimic the features and expressions of your miming behind your mask with your face. In this manner you will assume the proper mood and lend believablity to your actions.

6. When wearing a mask of a character with a double chin or impersonating a fat or short-necked person, hunch up the shoulders.

7. The body movements must express the character of the mask. Therefore, know the personality of the character by reading about him or her before pantomiming. Learn whether he or she was a calm, dignified, or excitable person. Know whether he or she was sly, clever, self-assured or skeptical.

A Word About Costumes and Sets

Professional mimics are able to assume any character without relying on costumes or sets. Most of them wear some sort of neutral costume. You may want to do this. However, for our purposes a very simple costume related to the character and just the suggestion of a set for atmosphere would not be out of place.

Sets used must be very simple and absolutely necessary for the action. If you feel confident in your ability to pantomime, try performing without the benefit of sets in any of the following stories, just as the real professionals do. Experiment and make your performance your very own creation.

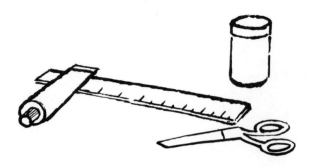

Pocahontas and
Captain John Smith

HISTORICAL BACKGROUND:
One of the most popular stories in American history is about
Pocahontas and how she saved the life of an early settler, Captain John Smith. Some historians believe it is a real story—
some, that it is made up. We do know that there was an Indian
girl, Pocahontas, whose name in Indian language—Matoaka—
meant "playful one." She was the daughter of a brave and powerful Indian chief, Powhatan. They lived in Jamestown, Vir-
ginia, at the time when our earliest settlers came to this country
from England in the early 1600's. Later John Rolfe, one of the
English settlers, fell in love with Pocahontas, and they were
married. They had a son and together they visited England
where Pocahontas was presented to the king and queen and
was received as a royal princess.

PRODUCTION NOTES:
The story that follows is meant for the young and is best enacted in the simplest pantomime. Pocahontas may be barefooted and wear a simple dress made of unbleached muslin
fringed at the hem and at the sleeves. Since she is the chief's

daughter, she wears a feather or two in her hair and a decorative band around her forehead. She is also adorned with a string of beads which can be made of strung macaroni. The barefooted women and girls may also wear tunics made of fringed, unbleached muslin but they do not wear feathers in their hair. The warriors' costumes may consist only of long trousers and a feather or two in their hair. They are barewaisted and barefooted and several carry drums. Their faces and bodies may be painted with different colors and designs. The barefooted Indian boys are in long trousers and are barewaisted but do not wear feathers. The Indian chief is the only one with a colorful blanket wrapped around him. The medicine men wear masks with streaks of red, black, and green painted on them in curious designs. Captain John Smith may wear long breeches, boots, and a tunic.

ACT I

At Curtain Rise:
We see a backdrop of an Indian village with tepees painted on it. Powhatan is seated before his tepee. Indian women and children are about. At the farthest corner there is much commotion.

Narrator: Captain John Smith, from the Jamestown Colony, is scouting the surrounding forest. He is set upon by a band of Indian hunters. They tie his arms and lead him to their village and Chief Powhatan. There are loud voices as the Indians enter the encampment with their prisoner. Women and children look in wonder and some fright at this strange individual for they have never seen a white man. But Pocahontas, Chief Powhatan's beautiful daughter, is not afraid. The warriors bring Captain John Smith before their chief and tell how they caught him. Chief Powhatan looks the prisoner over quietly. Then he calls out to his medicine men, who counsel him in serious tribal matters. Captain John Smith shows no fear as he stands before the chief. In fact, he looks about him with much curiosity. Then he sees several of the Indian warriors carrying stout clubs and knows he is in serious danger.

Chief Powhatan: Tell me, medicine men, what do your magic symbols say? What is to be done with this prisoner?

Narrator: The medicine men dance furiously to the rhythmic beat of drums. As they circle faster and faster they shout in loud tones to make their magic work. When they finally stop, one of the medicine men steps forward to speak to the chief.

Medicine Man: The Great Spirit of our magic has spoken. The white man brings evil upon our people. He must die.

Narrator: Chief Powhatan nods his head in agreement. Three Indian warriors step forward, each carrying a large stone. The stones are placed one upon another. Pocahontas knows what is about to take place. She has seen other captives forced to kneel before a mound of stones and rest their heads upon it. She has seen warriors bring their clubs down on the heads of captives and silence them forever.

Pocahontas: Father! Father! Do not kill the prisoner!

Narrator: Her voice is drowned out by the loud shouts of the warriors and villagers. Pocahontas then tugs at her father's robe. She catches his attention, but he looks away. Two Indians grab the Captain's arms and pull him toward the stones. The Captain does not resist. In fact, he walks proudly.

When the Indians try to push their prisoner to his knees, he does not permit them. He kneels by himself. He even places his head on the stones without help. Two Indians bearing huge clubs now walk to the side of the captive. They raise the clubs over the Captain's head. Just as they are about to lower them, Pocahontas rushes forward and throws herself across Captain John Smith's body. She places her head over his.

Pocahontas: No! No! You must not kill him! I will adopt him!

Narrator: The Indian executioners pause, with their clubs held high. Powhatan sees that his lovely daughter is in great danger.

Chief Powhatan: Do not strike! Pocahontas, what does this mean?

Narrator: The Indian warriors lower their clubs. Pocahontas turns to her father and speaks bravely.

Pocahontas: I, Pocahontas, daughter of the great Chief Powhatan, will adopt this man. You know it is the custom of our tribe that anyone wishing to adopt a captive may do so. You must grant me this wish. I claim it as my right!

Narrator: Powhatan looks at his daughter in silence for a long while. He can see that she is very serious. He also hears the medicine men grumbling at the delay of execution. At last the chief speaks.

Chief Powhatan: Very well, since it is your strong wish, the life of the prisoner will be spared. You may adopt him. We will make him a member of our tribe.

Narrator: Captain John Smith is then helped to his feet and his arms are freed. Pocahontas goes to him and extends her hand in friendship. So it was that Captain John Smith and the lovely Indian princess became good friends. (They walk off the stage together, hand in hand. Curtain closes.)

50

Paper Bag Mask

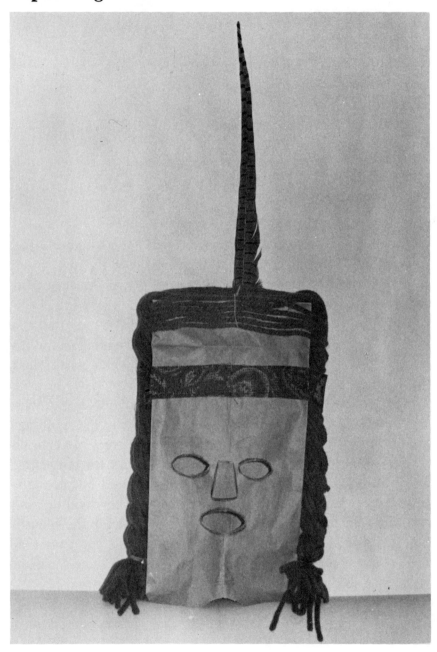

Materials:
brown paper bag
Jiffy Knit (thick black yarn) or black crepe paper
black crayon
small piece of colored construction paper
one or two large feathers
scissors
ruler
pencil
Elmer's Glue-All

Directions:
Facial Features:
1. Select a brown grocery bag that will fit over your head completely. Usually a number 20 bag will do (8 by 16 inches).
2. Draw a light pencil line down the middle of the bag. This will become your guideline for drawing in the features.
3. Open the bag and place it over your head. Be sure that the bottom of the bag rests comfortably on your shoulders. With your fingers, locate your eyes, nose, mouth, and ears. Mark these places very lightly with a pencil.
4. Remove the bag and lay it flat on a table. Draw in the eyes, nose, and mouth with a pencil. Be sure that the eye openings are on the same level, are the same size, and are large enough for seeing. On the vertical guideline mark a dot for the center of the bridge of the nose. Draw in the nose and be sure it is centered, equally spaced on both sides of the dividing line and large enough for breathing. Do the same for the mouth. Draw in the ear openings on the front part of the gusset of the bag (see sketch). Be sure they are on the same level on either side of the bag and large enough for hearing.
5. Open the bag and cut around the outline of the eyes, mouth, and ears with a scissor. To start the cuts, use the point of a

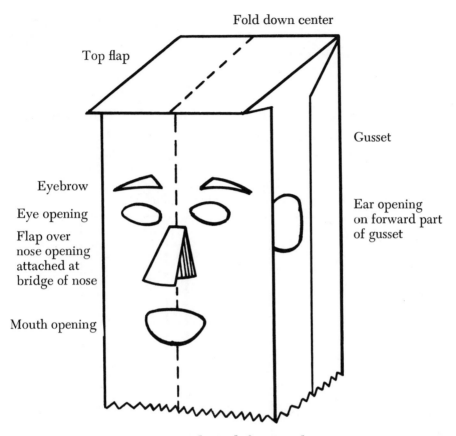

Fold down center

Top flap

Gusset

Eyebrow

Eye opening

Flap over
nose opening
attached at
bridge of nose

Ear opening
on forward part
of gusset

Mouth opening

Paper Bag Head Mask for Pocahontas

cuticle scissor. When you cut around the outline of the nose, leave the top (bridge) uncut (see sketch). Then you will be able to fit your nose through the opening so that the flap of paper covers it.

6. Redefine the eyes, nose, mouth, and ears with black crayon to make them more pronounced.

7. Open the paper bag, replace it over your head, and check to see if the openings are correctly placed and feel comfortable. If necessary, make corrections or start over again.

53

8. For eyebrows, cut two pieces of colored construction paper exactly alike (see sketch). Glue above each eye opening. Press to hold. Allow to dry.

Hair:

1. Open the top flap of the bag and measure the distance from the front of the bag to the back. This should be about 12 inches.
2. Cut three strips of masking tape, one inch wide and at least

Fold back ends of each strip
one-half inch at dotted lines

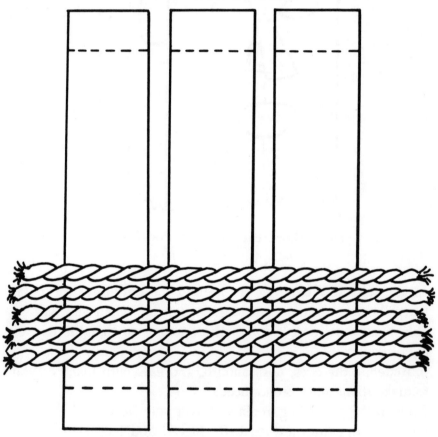

3 masking tape strips 1″ wide by 13″ long

Method for Construction Wig for Pocahontas

one inch longer than the above measurement. Lay each strip vertically, 1½ inches apart, flat on a table with the mucilage side up and the plain side down. Tuck under each end so that the mucilage will hold onto the table.

3. Measure and cut strips of Jiffy Knit, a thick black yarn, 56 inches long. Locate the center of a piece of yarn and lay it over the bottom of the center strip of masking tape (see sketch). Press to hold. Lay the rest of the strand of yarn over the left and right pieces of masking tape. Press to hold.

4. Proceed in the same manner with each strand of yarn, progressing upward over the three pieces of masking tape, until all of them have been covered.

5. Measure the length at the top of the bag from left to right. Add a few extra inches to this measurement to allow for the wig to fall slightly over each side of the bag. Then braid the strands of yarn from this point on each side. Use rubber bands to hold the ends of the braids (see sketch).

6. Open the bag and place it over a stand with a base.

7. Apply glue all over the top flap—around the four sides and center.

8. Lift the constructed wig off the table and center it over the top flap of the bag. Drape the wig over the front edge of the bag 1 to 2 inches. The braids will hang down at the sides. Tuck under the front and back pieces of masking tape. Apply a little glue on the front part of the bag (forehead) just under the wig, and press the yarn over it to hold. Gently press the wig over the whole flap to hold. Allow to dry. Now the unbraided part of the wig lays over the top of the flap, with a small part of it over the forehead, and the braids hang at either side of the face (see sketch).

9. To simulate a center part on the wig, use a piece of thin white yarn. Measure the depth (forehead to back) of the wig. Cut a piece of white yarn to that measurement. Use a dab of

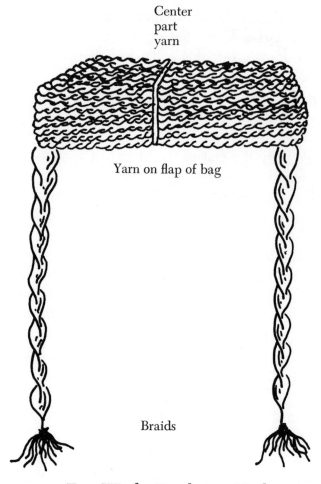

Center
part
yarn

Yarn on flap of bag

Braids

Yarn Wig for Pocahontas Mask

glue at one end of the white yarn and tuck it under the front center of the wig. Draw the rest of the yarn over the top of the wig and do the same with the other end.

10. For the headband across the forehead, use a strip of printed cloth (look in your scrap box) about 1½ inches wide and long enough to go around the bag (about 28 inches).

11. Apply glue over the wrong side of the headband. Find the

center of the headband and attach it across the forehead, over the braids, and all the way around the bag. Overlap the ends in the back if necessary. Press slightly to hold. Allow to dry. The headband is not only decorative but will help to hold the braids firmly in place.

The Boston Tea Party

HISTORICAL BACKGROUND:

In 1767 the English Parliament passed the Townshend Acts which taxed American colonists on imports of glass, lead, paints, paper, and tea. The colonists protested and the merchants boycotted English goods. The boycott decreased British trade, and in 1770 most of the Acts were repealed. The tax on tea was retained to prove to the colonists that they were still subject to the laws of the British government. But the colonists argued that the British government had no legal right to tax them, since they had no representation in Parliament. The colonists tried to prevent British merchants in America from accepting shipments of tea, and were successful in New York and Philadelphia. At Charleston the tea was unloaded from ships but held in government warehouses. At Boston the situation was different. A group of colonists called the Sons of Liberty showed their displeasure at the British government by impersonating the Mohawk Indians and dumping a shipload of tea overboard into the Boston Harbor. This incident is known as the Boston Tea Party.

The Mohawks used masks made of wood and cornhusks. They also used certain kinds of colored clay and stone ground fine and mixed with oil to make their face paint. The painting of faces was considered a form of magic to the Indians, as was the wearing of a mask. Every color had its own meaning. Red meant power; blue, defeat or trouble; white, peace; yellow—joy, travel or bravery. Black usually meant death or sorrow. The designs used were usually symbolic of animals, or the sky, the clouds, and the sun. It is probable that the colonists did not know all this and therefore used berries and vegetables native to their area for making the dyes to color their faces.

PRODUCTION NOTES:
The buckram mask is intended for the colonial spectators and their leaders. Those who board the ship to dump the tea are maskless. However, their faces and bodies are painted to represent the Mohawk Indians. They are dressed in trousers or blue jeans and are barefooted and barewaisted. They may wear feathers in their hair and each carries a small ax. Costumes for the colonists are not really necessary, but the men may wear tri-cornered hats and the women long skirts and a small cap of colonial design, if desired.

For sound effect, a whistle can be used as the tea is dumped overboard.

It would be fun to experiment with fruits and vegetables to make your own dye, just as the colonists did. Anything that grows in the garden or yard can be used as dye-stuff—flowers, vegetables, leaves, bark and twigs, nut hulls, berries and roots. For instance, beet juice creates a nice pinkish-red color and onion skin a soft orange or rust-orange. Yellows, apricots, and lime greens result from the use of twigs.

Dye materials should be gathered when the part of the plant to be used is at its most vital stage. Roots should be dug after the plant's growth has peaked. The best time to pick flowers is when they are coming into full bloom. Berries should be gathered when they are fully ripened. Leaves and bark should be collected in spring, although bark will also yield a good color if cut in the fall.

If it is not convenient to use the materials soon after they are gathered, they may be air-dried by placing them on wire mesh in a warm, dry place, so that air can circulate around them. Turn the material from time to time, to hasten the evaporation of moisture and prevent mildew. Or tie your materials into a small bunch and hang it upside down in a warm, dry place.

After drying, the material can be stored in a paper bag. Berries can be washed, stored in plastic bags or containers, and frozen. Flowers and leaves can also be frozen. When ready to be used, the plant materials should be soaked in water overnight and then boiled for one hour. Allow to cool and apply one color all over your face. When this has dried, apply other colors and create your own design. If natural materials are not available use watercolors, or lipstick and eye shadow.

ACT I

Scene I
At Curtain Rise:
We see a backdrop with a painted scene of the Boston Harbor and three sailing ships tied to the wharf. Also, the exterior of a warehouse is shown.

Narrator: A group of men and women are congregating and listening to a newsboy. He is carrying newspapers under one arm and waving another in his other hand, shouting as he walks up and down.

Newsboy: Extra! Extra! Read all about it! Three ships have

60

arrived from England loaded with tea. They are tied at Griffin's wharf. The tea is taxed at threepence a pound. Extra! Extra! Ships with tea have also arrived in New York, Philadelphia and Charleston. Extra! Extra! Read all about it!

Narrator: Some spectators buy a newspaper and read briefly while the newsboy continues to shout the news. One spectator waves his fist with annoyance.

First Spectator: Great Britain has certainly tried our patience. First it was the sugar tax; then the Stamp Act. Imagine having to buy a stamp for every piece of printed paper we use, just to keep King George's treasury well supplied.

Second Spectator: And now a tax on the one drink a poor man enjoys—tea.

Third Spectator: I say we must learn to live without it rather than pay the tax.

Fourth Spectator: How *can* we live without it?

Narrator: There is mounting excitement. The men and women are heard shouting.

First Spectator: We *must* live without it! We must not pay the tax no matter how much we want the tea. It's a matter of principle. Now the tea tax, next it will be something else. There will be no end to it.

Narrator: Now all are extremely angry.

Second Spectator: King George has no right to do this to us. We don't even have representation in his Parliament.

Third Spectator: I say, no taxation without representation.

All Together: Hear! Hear!

Fourth Spectator: Let's go right now to merchant Clark at the warehouse and demand that he not unload the tea from the ships.

Narrator: They all shout together, waving their arms.

Spectators: Aye! Aye! To the warehouse! To the warehouse! (They exit together. Curtain closes.)

Scene II

We see the same backdrop with a group of colonists congregated in front of it.

Narrator: Richard Clark, a merchant and owner of the warehouse, is faced by an angry group of colonists. They have come as a committee to protest the arrival of the cargo of tea, and especially the tax on it.

First Committee Member: Richard Clark, we're here to speak for the people of Boston. We ask you to promise not to sell the cargo of tea just arrived and in your charge.

Second Committee Member: We demand that you send the chests of tea back to London unopened.

Narrator: Clark becomes annoyed and angry.

Clark: I want nothing to do with you. You have no right to speak in this manner. Leave my warehouse!

Third Committee Member: We have the right of an oppressed people.

Clark: I have nothing to do with governmental matters. I suggest you speak to Governor Hutchinson.

Narrator: Clark makes a quick exit. (Curtain closes.)

ACT II

At Curtain Rise:

We see the interior of the Old Meeting House. There is a table with a candle on it and chairs about.

Narrator: Several men are grouped around Samuel Adams. Angry voices sound throughout the room. Suddenly Francis Rotch, a shipowner, enters. All look to him for news.

Rotch: Gentlemen, as you suggested I spoke to the Governor about a clearance to sail my ship back to England with the tea.

Adams: What was his reply?

Rotch: The Governor firmly refused. The ships will be unloaded in the morning.

Narrator: Excited and angry voices are heard throughout the group. Samuel Adams stands on a chair and signals for quiet. He tries to restore order.

Adams: Gentlemen, this meeting can do nothing more to save the country.

Narrator: One spectator is heard shouting, then another.

First Spectator: Who knows how tea will mingle with salt water?

Second Spectator: Boston Harbor will be a teapot tonight! The Mohawks will come!

Narrator: They all exit shaking their fists, shouting angrily, and repeating the refrain. (Curtain closes.)

Act III

At Curtain Rise:

It is nighttime and the stage is in semi-darkness. The backdrop is the harbor scene. We see a platform the length of the stage which represents the deck of the ship. There are several chests or large boxes filled with tea on the platform. The boxes may or may not have small dried leaves or bits of torn paper in them. A railing marks the edge of the deck, and a tall mast and rigging may be in the center.

Narrator: Two disguised Mohawks sneak about the wharf looking from left to right, then jump over the rail, and board the ship. They approach the boxes of tea stacked in the corner. One of the men grabs a box and passes it to his companion.

First Disguised Mohawk: Heave ho!

Narrator: The second disguised Mohawk opens the box with his ax and empties the contents over the rail.

Second Disguised Mohawk: And over she goes!

Narrator: The disguised Mohawks work as a team. One passes a box of tea to the other, who opens it and empties the contents over the rail.

Disguised Mohawks Together: And over she goes!

Narrator: The boatswain's whistle is heard again as groups of people assemble to see what is taking place. As each box is dumped into the harbor, the people cheer loudly. Box after box of tea is opened and disposed of in this manner. At last, when all the tea is dumped overboard, the disguised Mohawks jump over the rail. In high spirits, they place their axes over their shoulders and march away to the tune of "Yankee Doodle." The spectators follow, knowing that the Boston Tea Party is only the beginning of their efforts to establish a free and independent nation. (Curtain closes.)

Buckram Mask

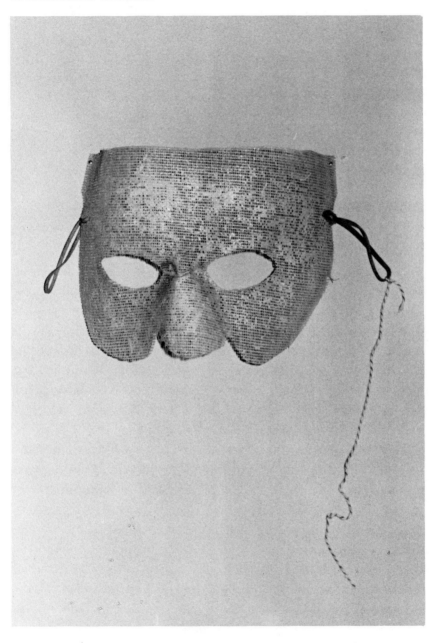

Materials:
½ yard buckram (can be obtained from a dry goods store)
wrapping paper
scissors
pencil
sponge
tempera poster paints—white, light red, yellow, blue
small paint brush
Scotch tape
small mixing pan

Directions:
1. To make a mask which fits an average size face, trace the pattern shown here on a sheet of plain typing paper. Do not press too hard with your pencil or you will tear the paper. Lift the paper from the pattern. Cut along the solid lines, including the eye. Since this is only a half pattern, fold a piece of wrapping paper lengthwise. Lay the straight edge of the drawing on the fold of the wrapping paper and trace around the pattern. Remove the pattern and cut around the contour and eye opening of the doubled paper. Open it. Now you have a full size pattern for the buckram mask. Check it against your face and make any necessary adjustments or corrections.
2. To make a pattern for a mask to fit your own face, measure the length of your face from the hairline to the bottom of your nose and from temple to temple. Cut a piece of wrapping paper using these measurements.
3. Place the paper against your face or else have someone else do it for you. With a pencil, outline the contour for only half the face, from temple to cheek line, then across the front of the face to under the nose (follow shapes of pattern illustrated).
4. Remove the paper from your face. Fold it in half lengthwise and redefine the outline as shown in the illustrated pattern.

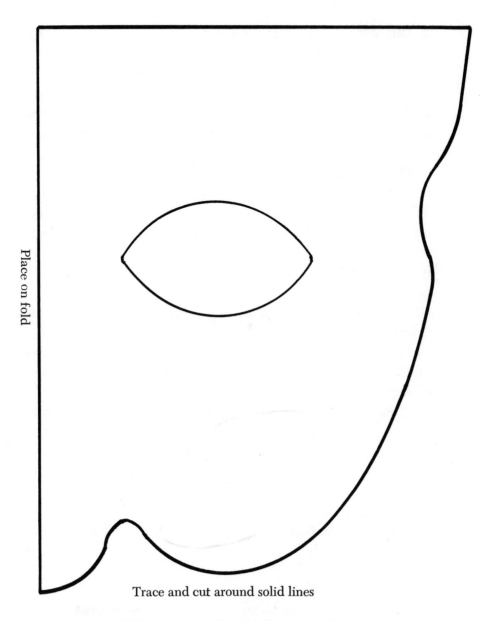

Place on fold

Trace and cut around solid lines

Full Size Pattern for Buckram Mask

5. Cut around this pattern line. Open the paper. Now you have a symmetrically-shaped mask. Check it against your face for any necessary corrections.

6. Fold a piece of buckram in half lengthwise. Fold the paper pattern and place the fold on the fold of the buckram. Trace around the buckram with a pencil. Remove the pattern and cut around the contour of the buckram.

7. Open the buckram and check it against your face for size.

8. With a wet sponge, dampen both sides of the buckram.

9. Lay the buckram against your face, or else have someone else do it for you. Press it carefully and firmly with your fingers so it molds over your features. Since buckram is highly starched, it will take the imprint and form of your face—the cheekbones, nose, temples, and eye sockets.

10. Keep the buckram against your face for a few minutes until it becomes dry.

11. Before removing the mask, outline the eye openings with black crayon. Be sure they are on the same level and large enough to see through.

12. Remove the buckram from your face. Crumble a piece of paper toweling and lay the buckram over it. This will help the mask to retain its shape until thoroughly dry.

13. Insert the point of a cuticle scissor through one corner of the eye and cut around. Do the same for the other eye opening.

14. Check the mask against your face and make any necessary corrections. Note how this type of mask allows your mouth and jaw to move freely.

Painting the Mask:

1. Mix a little light red and yellow and a good deal of white tempera paint in a mixing pan. This will become the basic skin color for the mask.

2. Apply this mixture moderately to the mask with a paint-

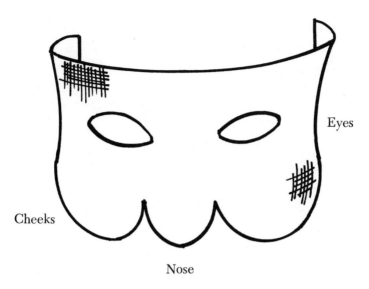

Eyes

Cheeks

Nose

Mask for the Boston Tea Party

brush. Do not allow the buckram to become too wet or it will lose its shape.

3. To achieve halftones for the forehead, cheeks, and nose, add more of one color or another to the basic skin color in the mixing pan and apply to the mask. Mix a tiny bit of blue to the basic skin color for dark shadows on either side of the nose. Use more white on the forehead since this area will catch highlights. Use a little more red for the high points of the cheeks and a darker tone for the temples. Experiment with your paints as much as you like.

4. When the mask has been painted to your satisfaction, place it again over the crumbled paper toweling and allow it to dry thoroughly. If the mask loses its shape in the drying process, moisten your fingers with water and press the shape back to its original form.

5. Bind the edge of the mask with a narrow piece of Scotch

tape so that half of the tape covers the front edge and half the back edge. This will protect your face from scratching by the rough edge of the buckram and will add to the durability of the mask. Trim curves and corners where necessary.

6. Attach rubber bands and string as directed and illustrated in "Some Things To Consider in Mask-Making," step number 14, page 37. Now you are ready to wear your mask for *The Boston Tea Party*.

This mask can also be made with aluminum foil and tinted with inks or colored felt marking pens.

Harriet Tubman, Conductor of the Freedom Train

HISTORICAL BACKGROUND:
Harriet Tubman was born a slave on a plantation in Eastern Tidewater, Maryland in 1820. She was a remarkable woman of great strength, courage, and religious feelings who fervently believed that, "The Lord did not intend for people to be slaves."

Harriet repeatedly risked her life leading small groups of runaway slaves to freedom. She took them through the woods and across the waters of Maryland, Delaware, Pennsylvania, New York and finally to Canada, aided along the way by kindly Dutch Quakers and abolitionists. She was considered the conductor, and those she guided the passengers, of the underground railroad which ran to the North and freedom. In reality, it was not a "railroad" at all, but a group of people who offered food, shelter, and a temporary hiding place to fugitive slaves seeking their freedom.

Harriet's people thought of her as a Moses. She would go to a southern plantation in the dark of night, and announce her arrival in the slaves' quarters by singing softly behind their doors, "Go down Moses, way down to Egypt land." "Moses has come, Moses is here," they would whisper, and preparations were quickly made by those who wished to steal away with her in the dark of night.

It is not known exactly how many slaves Harriet led to freedom. A figure of more than 400 is often mentioned. Long after the Civil War when the slaves had won their freedom, Harriet would recall those dark, dangerous days and say, "On my underground railroad, I never ran my train off the track and I never lost a passenger."

PRODUCTION NOTES:
The action in the story takes place mainly in a wooded area. No elaborate props are necessary since the story is told by the narrator and the action is mimed. You may simply use a backdrop with a painted scene of a forest and a farmhouse in the distance. A few branches of shrubbery are placed here and there on the stage. No special costumes are necessary but if desired, the slave women could wear simple loose garments made of unbleached muslin or old sheets. The slave men could wear dungarees and be shirtless. The slaves are barefooted. Have as few or as many slaves in the group as desired. The Quaker women may be dressed in long gathered skirts and blouses and wear bonnets. The Quaker men may have sideburns and beards of black tinted cotton, and wear broad black hats, trousers, and white shirts. Use a flashlight for the light which is seen in the last farmhouse. Be sure to have sound effects of the owl, whippoorwill, horses' hooves, night creatures, snapping of twigs, etc. where needed.

ACT I

Scene I
At Curtain Rise:
We see a backdrop of a painted wooded area with a farmhouse

at a distant corner. Sets of shrubbery are placed here and there on the stage.

Narrator: Several slave men and women are working in a cotton field. A young slave girl is picking cotton and singing in a sad, rich voice.

Slave Girl: *Nobody knows the trouble I see*
Nobody knows but Jesus
Nobody knows the trouble I see
Glory hallelujah

Narrator: A white woman walks near by. She stops and looks at the attractive black girl who is working. She listens for a while to the sad song.

White Woman: What is your name?

Narrator: The young girl straightens up and looks at the woman.

Slave Girl: Harriet, Ma'm, but they call me Hat.

White Woman: Why are you so sad, Harriet?

Harriet: We have a new master, Ma'm. We're afraid he will sell us to another plantation owner, and we will be separated from our families.

Narrator: The white woman starts to walk away and without even glancing at Harriet, she speaks.

White Woman: If ever you need any help, come to see me. I am a Quaker and live on a farm near Bucktown.

Narrator: The woman leaves and Harriet continues her work and song. A slave laboring close to Harriet beckons to her. Harriet, bending over as though working, slowly makes her way towards him. The man whispers to her.

Slave Man: The water boy has just brought us news that you have been sold to a Georgia trader and will be sent South tomorrow morning.

Narrator: Harriet keeps on working as if nothing unusual is happening. Then she stands up straight and looks to the sky.

Harriet: Lord, I'm going to hitch my wagon to you. You've got to see me through.

Scene II

Narrator: The slaves keep on working. At evening time, when the work in the field is done, Harriet and the other slaves go back to their living quarters. Shortly after dark, Harriet steals quietly out of her cabin. It is dark, but she knows her way. She stops at a few cabins, knocks at the doors, and whispers.

Harriet: *Go down Moses*
Way down in Egypt's land
Tell old Pharaoh
Let my people go

Narrator: One by one the cabin doors open just enough to let a person through. In this way, Harriet gathers a small group of companions who long to be free. The small band makes its way through the woods, often stumbling over tangled vines on the ground. From time to time they hear the sound of horses' hoofs. This could only mean that their plantation owner is out looking for them. Harriet and her small group hide under the brush. Their fear is worse than their hunger. They know that if they are caught, they will be brought back and whipped, then sold and taken in chains to plantations in the deep South. So they stay hidden until the sound of horses' hooves grows fainter and finally disappears altogether. They journey onward.

First Slave Woman: Where are you taking us, Harriet?

Harriet: To Bucktown, where the white woman who talked to me in the field lives. I'm not sure that she will keep us all. But we'll soon find out.

Narrator: The group travels on as quickly as it can. When it finally reaches the farmhouse in Bucktown, Harriet motions to her followers to hide in the surrounding brush. She circles

74

the house slowly, then walks to the door, and taps gently on it.

Voice from Within: Who is there?

Harriet: A friend and I bring friends.

Narrator: The door opens slowly. The white woman recognizes Harriet and with a quick wave of her hand, beckons them all to come in.

Scene III

Narrator: The Quaker woman feeds the runaway slaves. Then she gives Harriet a piece of paper with the names of two people to whom the group can go for refuge. After that the slaves lay down on the floor and sleep.

The next night the woman's husband leads Harriet and her small band of runaway slaves out into the darkness. After guiding them for a while, the Quaker points the direction in which they are to continue their journey. Then he turns around and disappears into the darkness.

Once again, Harriet leads her small band of runaways, climbing over tangled vines and brushwood. They freeze with fear when an owl hoots or the whippoorwill calls.

First Slave Man: Harriet, I'm going back. I'm going back, Harriet. They'll surely catch us.

Narrator: Harriet stops and faces the frightened runaway.

Harriet: You'll do no such thing. You know what will happen to you if you go back. They'll thrash and beat you until you tell them where we are. Then they'll find us and whip us to an inch of our lives, chain us, and march us to the deep South. You have one of two choices. Either you die a freeman or you die a slave. Which will it be?

Narrator: After this, they all know that they must push on and take their chances for freedom. On they go under cover of night. At last they reach the edge of the woods, tired and hungry. A short distance away they see a white farmhouse.

This is the Quaker house where they are to stop on the second lap of their journey. Harriet taps gently on the door while her companions gather around her.

Voice from Within: Who is there?

Harriet: A friend with friends.

Narrator: A Quaker man opens the door cautiously and then signals them to come in. The Quaker's wife feeds the hungry runaway slaves. Then they are made comfortable on the floor where they sleep the rest of the night and all day.

Scene IV

Narrator: That night the runaways go out of the house one by one. The Quaker man stands at the door and points in the direction they are to take.

Quaker Man: Go through the woods and watch for a farmhouse with a light in the window. Go quickly, and may you have a safe journey.

Narrator: The Quaker closes the door and once again the runaway slaves are led by the courageous girl who would rather die than turn back. They push on, stumbling in the woods. Now that they are on their last lap to freedom, they are more afraid that they may be caught. Each snap of a broken twig or sound of a night creature sends them to cover. They become so tired they can hardly walk. Harriet, far ahead of the rest, turns back to urge them on.

Harriet: Faster, faster, hurry, hurry.

First Slave: Harriet, what if there is no light in the window? What if it is a trick to catch us?

Second Slave: Why do these free people want to help us?

Harriet: Could it be because they too believe that people are not born to be slaves?

Narrator: The runaways trudge on, weary and cautious. Suddenly they see a faint light shining in the distance. As they get closer to it they see that there *is* a light in a window, just as the Quaker had said there would be. The band of tired, hungry runaway slaves gather before the farmhouse. Freedom is now but a short distance away. At last, they will be free! They lift their arms high and sing out:

Lord, blow your trumpet!
Awaken this Nation!
Lord, blow your trumpet!
Hallelujah! Hallelujah!

(Curtain closes.)

Construction Paper Mask

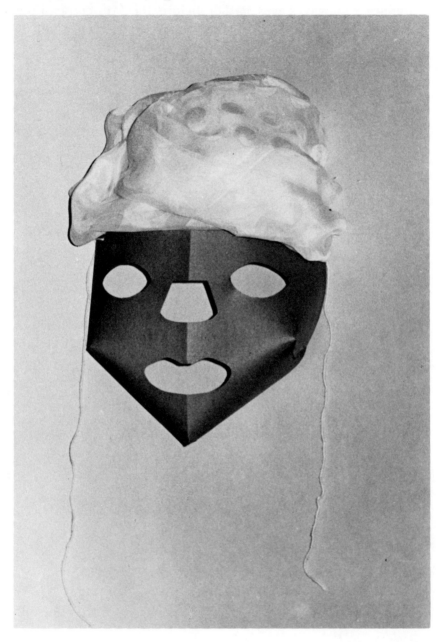

Materials:

wrapping paper 10 inches by 14 inches for a basic pattern
brown construction paper 10 inches by 14 inches for a finished
  mask
long white scarf or crepe paper about 17 inches by 40 inches
  for a bandanna
scissors
ruler
tape measure
pencil
Elmer's Glue-All

Directions:

Basic Pattern:

1. Measure a piece of wrapping paper (or newspaper) 10 inches by 14 inches and cut to size. If you do not have either, a large grocery bag cut open will do. The 14 inch side is for the width of the mask and the 10 inch side for the length.
2. Fold the paper in half lengthwise.
3. To shape the mask, measure the distance from the edge of your hairline to a little below the bottom of your chin with a tape measure. Indicate this measurement with pencil lines on the paper. This will become the length of the mask. In the same manner, measure the distance from ear to ear and indicate this on the paper. This will be the width of the mask. Draw your facial contour from these measurements (see sketch.)
4. For features, measure the distance from the edge of your hairline to the bridge of your nose and indicate this with a pencil line on the pattern. Measure the length of your nose and indicate this on the pattern. Measure the distance from your hairline to your lips and indicate this on the pattern. Measure the distance of the outer corner of your eye to the inner corner and mark this width on the pattern with pencil lines.

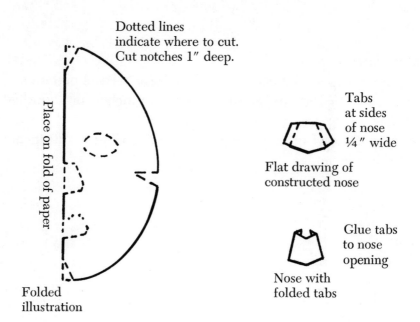

Dotted lines indicate where to cut. Cut notches 1″ deep.

Place on fold of paper

Folded illustration

Tabs at sides of nose ¼″ wide

Flat drawing of constructed nose

Glue tabs to nose opening

Nose with folded tabs

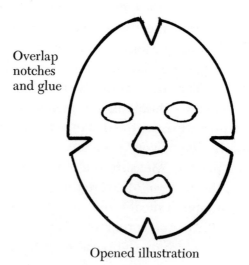

Overlap notches and glue

Opened illustration

Construction for Harriet Tubman Mask

5. Draw in the features and be sure the eye and half the nose and mouth are large enough.

6. Keeping the pattern folded, cut around the contour of the face.

7. Insert the point of a cuticle scissors into one corner of the eye and cut around it. Cut out the half nose and mouth. (See the labeled illustration.)

8. Open the pattern. The sides will be symmetrical.

9. Check the mask against your face and be sure that all the openings are large enough and fit comfortably over your own facial features. If not, start over again, making necessary corrections until the mask is right.

Finished Mask:

1. Fold a brown piece of construction paper 10 inches by 14 inches. If you do not have construction paper, cut open a large brown grocery bag and cut to size.

2. Fold in half lengthwise, the same as the pattern.

3. Fold the basic pattern in half lengthwise and place the fold over the fold of the construction paper.

4. Trace around the pattern.

5. Trace feature openings. Remove pattern.

6. Cut around the contour of the construction paper. Cut out features.

7. Open the construction paper.

8. Cut notches at forehead, chin, and cheeks one inch deep as shown in the illustration. Glue and overlap notches. Press to hold. Allow to dry. Now your mask has the depth to fit over your face.

9. For the nose, either leave the opening as is (this is recommended for more comfort in breathing) or add a constructed piece over the opening. To do this, use the nose cutout piece (shown in the illustration) as a guide. Since right and left tabs

will be required to attach it over the nose opening, be sure to make it wider than the cutout piece on the mask. Draw a structure on brown construction paper, similar to the illustration in the book. Fold your drawing in half lengthwise and redefine the drawing. Cut around the outline. Open the constructed nose. Draw in the dotted lines for the left and right tabs. Fold along the dotted lines. Put glue along the tabs on right and left side of the nose. Attach it to the mask opening so that the bridge of the nose lies between the eyes. Be sure that the fold down the center comes slightly away from the mask, thus giving depth to the nose. Press to hold. Allow to dry.

10. To attach the mask to your face, place it over your face to fit comfortably. Carefully mark dots at either side of the temples near the edges. Remove the mask from your face and with a sharp tool (the point of a cuticle scissors will do) make a hole large enough for a strong piece of string. To reinforce each hole, attach a piece of masking tape on the inner side of the mask close to the edge and redefine the openings. Insert a piece of strong string through each hole and tie. Note that with this mask you should not use rubber bands which might tear the paper when it is stretched. When the mask is ready to be worn, simply tie the two pieces of string at the back of your head.

11. Now your mask is ready to be worn with a white bandanna draped around your head.

Where There is No North

HISTORICAL BACKGROUND:

Commodore Robert E. Peary's greatest ambition in life was to be the first man to reach the North Pole. He was urged on purely by the spirit of adventure. Peary was not interested in finding a new travel route through the Arctic region as were other explorers before him.

In preparation for his dash to the North Pole, Peary made a series of seven learning expeditions to the Arctic. He got to know the Eskimos and their ways of living in the harsh, often cruel, Arctic world. Peary felt that the combination of his technical skill as a naval officer and the Eskimos' knowledge of how to survive in the frozen Arctic would assure a successful march to the Pole.

In July of 1908, Peary left the United States for his great adventure. He sailed on the *Roosevelt*, a ship built especially for battling ice floes. In the fall, the explorer and his party finally reached Cape Sheridan on the tip of northern Greenland. Leaving the ship at this point, Peary set out with a large group of men, supplies, and equipment for Cape Columbia, the northern edge of Ellesmere Land. His purpose was to establish a base camp from which he would start out on his trek to the North Pole. But first a trail had to be marked and supply depots set up along the route.

With the help of 17 Eskimos, 5 white men, Peary's ever-faithful black friend, Matthew Henson, and 133 Eskimo sled dogs, the work of finding a good trail north began. Five different parties, working in relays with their dogs and sleds, set out to break a trail over the barren ice. Each of the parties established igloo camps at about 50 mile intervals, stocked them with supplies, then returned to the base camp at Ellesmere Land. When one party returned, another would start, use the established camps, then extend the trail and establish another support camp about 50 miles further north. The fifth and last support camp was set up about 130 miles from the Pole.

From this point Peary planned to make his dash to the North Pole. He started on his march northward. His companions were Henson, and four Eskimos, Ootah, Ooqueah, Egingwah, and Seegloo. They traveled with 5 supply sleds pulled by 40 dogs.

The journey was not easy. There were many perils and the weather was bitterly cold. Huge blocks of ice barred the way. Often there was no way to go but over them. Then the men, slipping and falling, pushed or pulled their heavy sleds to help the dogs get over the obstacles. There were dangerous cracks in the ice, open water leads to cross. This took extra care because a fall into icy water could mean instant death.

Finally, on April 6, 1909, Robert E. Peary knew from his navigation instruments that he had reached his goal. The men cheered as they stood together where North, East, South and West meet at one point on the top of the earth.

PRODUCTION NOTES:
Outdoor clothes are worn throughout by the men and women. The Eskimo women can be seen making clothing in true panto-mime fashion, and the Eskimo men assembling the sleds with

84

thongs. Although sled dogs are never seen, their barks should be heard as sound affects at appropriate times. An American flag could be used in the last act.

ACT I

At Curtain Rise:
We see a painted backdrop of ice floes and mounds of ice and snow. A group of Eskimo men and Peary's expedition party are seen together.

Narrator: When the Eskimos hear that Admiral Peary has once again arrived in their midst, they are overjoyed to see him. They know that Peary has returned for another attempt to find the North Pole. After shaking hands with the Eskimos, Peary begins to select the ones who will accompany him on the trek to the Pole. He questions each man.

Peary: Do you have good, strong sled dogs?

First Eskimo: We have good husky dogs.

Peary: Can you build extra long, strong sleds? I will need many of them.

Second Eskimo: Our good friend from the South land must know that we build the strongest and best sleds in the North.

Narrator: Peary nods and then begins to pick Eskimos to accompany him. All are delighted to be part of the American explorer's expedition. They know the journey will not be easy but they want to go anyway. They slap one another on the back and talk excitedly among themselves. (Curtain closes.)

ACT II

The Preparation
At Curtain Rise:
Four Eskimo women are seated together on the floor sewing clothing to be worn by Peary's North Pole party.

Narrator: Peary arrives, carrying patterns of caribou fur suits. He cut the patterns himself and now they are to be sewn. One of the Eskimo women rises and takes the patterns from Peary. Then she returns to her place with the others.

Eskimo Woman: We must first chew the edge of the caribou skins to make them soft before we sew them.

Narrator: Each woman takes a fur pattern and begins chewing around it with her teeth. Peary leaves them with their work. When the tough skins are pliable enough, the women begin to sew, making trousers, jackets, parkas and mittens. These will be worn by Peary and his companions on their march North. Soon the Eskimo men join them—Ootah, Ooqueah, Egingwah and Seegloo. Each carries parts of a long, narrow sled which Peary designed especially for the journey over the ice.

Ootah: These sleds will be better than any we have made.

Ooqueah: Our leader knows well that the sleds must be extra long and strong to span breaks in the ice.

Narrator: The Eskimo men bind the parts of the sleds together with long, leather thongs as the women continue sewing. Peary enters.

Peary: Ootah, Ooqueah, Egingwah, Seegloo, be sure to make the sleds strong. Then find the ablest, strongest, and most courageous dogs you have to pull them. The dogs will be our lifeline to help us reach the place where there is No North. And I am depending on you to manage and care for them.

Egingwah: We will help you as we have before, only this time we will reach the place where there is No North.

Peary: You must not forget to hunt for fresh meat to take with us.

Seegloo: We will do that too.

Ootah: We will be sure to beg the pardon of our relative, the caribou, before we kill him for food. This is our custom.

86

Narrator: Peary nods his head, for he understands the Eskimos' feeling that at death their spirits will take on the forms of animals. Peary leaves, and the Eskimos continue their work. (Curtain closes.)

ACT III

The Loading and Briefing

At Curtain Rise:

The North Pole party consisting of Eskimos, Henson, white men and Peary is seen.

Narrator: Peary calls out as the men carry packages and bundles to the sleds.

Peary: Pemmican, dried ground buffalo meat, our most important food for men and dogs. Some fresh caribou meat. Now tea and condensed milk. Alcohol stoves to heat the tea. Let's not forget the fur blankets.

Narrator: The men carry and tie the packed items to the sleds. Excitement mounts. In the distance the loud barking of the spirited Eskimo dogs can be heard. Somehow the animals know that they are part of the preparations and so are anxious to start their journey. When the packing is finished, Peary inspects the sleds to his satisfaction. He gathers his men about him and tells them about his plan for the expedition.

Peary: My plan is to have five supporting sled parties. Each sled is to be led by a white man with three Eskimos and the pulling dogs. The first supporting party will start from our home base, travel for about 50 miles if possible, and make camp. You are to construct an igloo and leave supplies in it. Then you are to return to home base with enough supplies to see you safely back. A second supporting party will start out from home base and travel over the same trail. This party will use the camp established by the first party, then push on for another 50 miles. At this point the second party will also build an igloo, leave supplies, and return to home base with enough food for themselves. A third, fourth, and fifth supporting party will do the same, each time pushing on further than the last supporting group. I will start out last with Henson and four Eskimos. When I reach the last support camp, I will use it as a take-off point for the final lap to the Pole. We must start now and return before the spring thaw arrives. If the weather becomes too warm it will make the movement of the ice towards the sea too perilous for travel. How do you feel about this plan?

Henson: We are here only to help you reach the North Pole. If you think what you have just told us is the best way of reaching that goal, then we will follow. If necessary, we are prepared to spend a year or two longer to find the Pole. But I feel this won't be necessary. This time we will reach the North Pole.

Ootah: We trust you. Where you lead, we are ready to go.

Peary: We leave behind us everything that we love; family, home, and friends. Ahead of us lies the dream, the goal which has escaped me for twenty-three years. The No land of the Great North. From now on we shall be dependent only upon ourselves while struggling against the elements of Nature.

Narrator: All the men shake hands and bid one another farewell. Soon the first of the advance parties departs northward. (Curtain closes.)

ACT IV

The Dash to the North Pole
At Curtain Rise:
We see Peary and his party consisting of Henson, Ootah, Egingwah, Seegloo and Ooqueah, gathered together.

Narrator: The last of the support teams has completed its mission and has returned safely to the base camp at Cape Columbia. Peary with his party and five sleds packed with food and supplies has arrived at the fifth and last of the support bases. At this base, about one hundred and thirty miles from the North Pole, Peary and his companions rest. Sleds are inspected and repairs made where needed. Equipment is checked for the last time. Finally all is ready. The moment for the final dash has arrived. This is the time for which Peary has reserved the last of his energy; the time for which he had trained himself as if preparing for a foot-race. Peary and his five companions head straight north. From time to time, Peary stops and checks his compass. They are in a region where no human being has ever been before. Peary strains his eyes into the whiteness ahead. He dashes ahead of his companions, fearing that there might be an open water lead just ahead. Peary sighs with relief to see nothing but endless reaches of ice, and the men follow when he signals with a wave of his arm that all is clear.

While the other men pause to rest and eat, Peary checks their progress. He wants to find out how far north they have traveled since leaving support base number Five. They could be very close to the North Pole—perhaps they may even have arrived. Using his navigation sextant for sighting the sun, Peary calculates their longitude and latitude. Suddenly he lets out a shout.

Peary: The Pole! The Pole at last! We're standing at the top of the world where there is no North.

All Shout Together: We're here, we're here at last!

Narrator: Peary removes an American flag which is wrapped around his body under his outer jacket. One of the Eskimos brings a pole and some tools from a sled and nails the flag to it. All together they raise the flag as a symbol of their victory. They give three rousing cheers and then Peary shakes hands with each member of the party. He thanks them warmly for all their help. They slap each other's backs as an expression of success. The explorers are tired but happy for having reached the long elusive goal. (Curtain closes.)

Papier-Mâché Mask

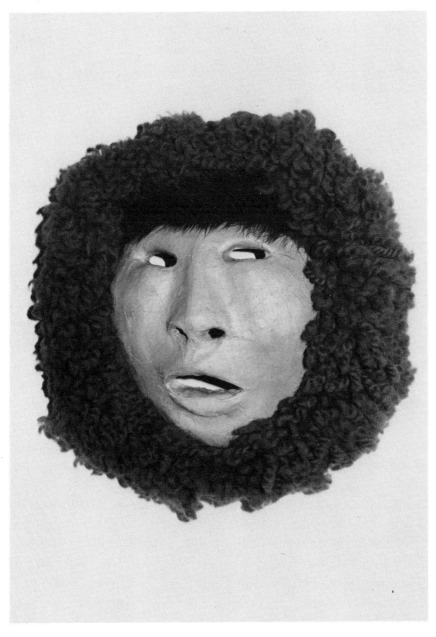

Making the Mold
Materials:
5 pounds of moist modeling clay or Plasticine
bowl, 9 inches in diameter, 4 inches deep
wooden tongue depressor, or broad handled tablespoon
wooden board, about 14 inches by 11 inches
tape measure
Saran Wrap or wax paper

Directions:
1. Cover your work table with newspaper. Place the wooden board on it and turn the bowl upside down over the board.
2. Cover the bowl with Saran Wrap, or wax paper, so that it overhangs onto the board (see photograph). It may be necessary to use more than one piece to cover all of the bowl.
3. Take a large piece of clay and flatten it like a large, thick pancake. Use a rolling pin if you have one, otherwise your hands will do. Lay it over the bowl. It may be necessary to add to the clay in order to cover the whole bowl. Be sure the clay hangs over the bowl onto the wooden board. This will anchor the bowl and prevent it from moving as you work with the mold.
4. Measure the length of your face from a little above the hairline to just below the chin with a tape measure. Measure the width of your face from a little beyond one temple to the other.
5. With the edge of a wooden tongue depressor, or the handle of a tablespoon, mark off on the clay the length of your face from hairline to chin, and the width from temple to temple. Use the tool as you would a pencil. Now you have marked off the correct length and width of the mask to fit your face.
6. With the edge of the depressor, draw into the clay the contour of your face from hairline to chin on both sides. Again

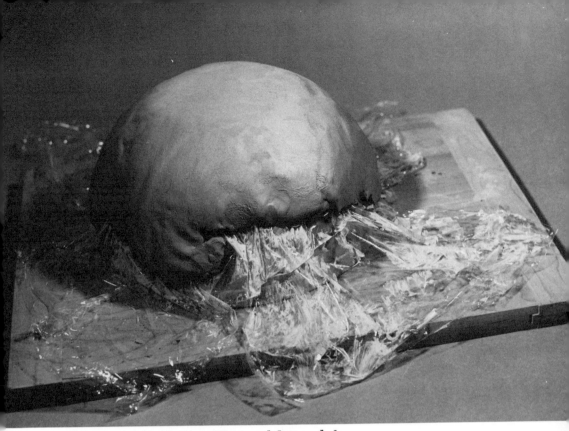

Bowl covered with Saran Wrap and flattened clay.

Bowl completely covered with clay.

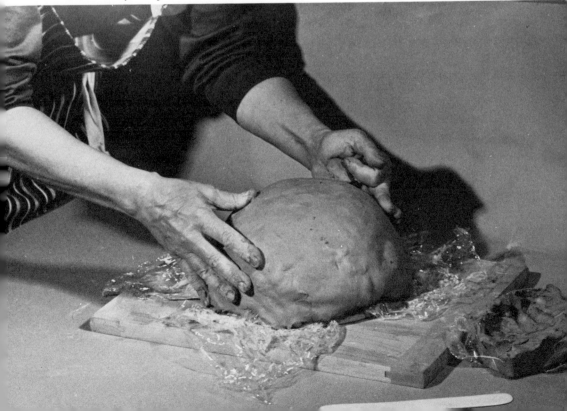

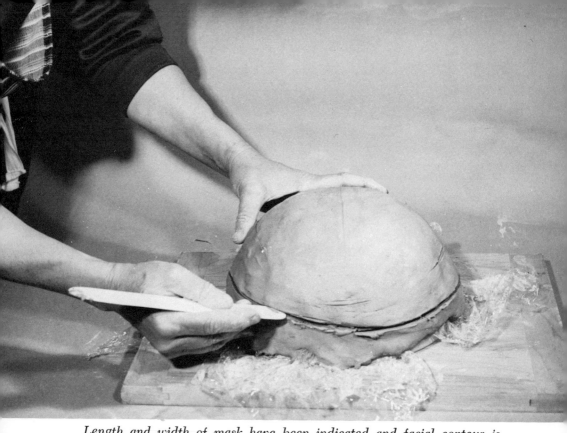

Length and width of mask have been indicated and facial contour is defined with the edge of a tongue depressor tool.

Facial features are scribed on clay with a tongue depressor tool.

use the tool as though you were drawing with a pencil. Since the mask is to be an Eskimo's face, be sure to make the contour broad and round.

7. With a tape measure, measure the placement of your facial features—from hairline to eye level, from hairline to the tip of the nose, from hairline to the mouth. Mark these measurements by scribing a line on the clay, using the edge of a tongue depressor tool. Measure the size of your eye and mouth and mark these on the clay in a similar way. Now draw the features on the clay, using the depressor tool as you would a pencil. The correct placement and size of your features on the clay will result in a mask to fit your very own face. The finished mask should be comfortable for seeing, breathing, and speaking.

8. When you are satisfied with the position of the facial features, use the edge of the tongue depressor to lift out the eye openings, and the mouth opening.

9. From here on, sculpting with clay is a matter of adding or subtracting clay. But mostly, small pieces are added bit by bit, until you have shaped the facial features to your satisfaction. Be sure to add clay for the nose, upper and lower lip, cheekbones, and eyebrow structures. With your fingers, feel the bone and muscle structures on both sides of your face for symmetry. This will tell you where to add or subtract clay. You will discover that your thumbs are very strong and serviceable for adding and smoothing.

10. With the tongue depressor, mark off the nostril openings and push up this part of the clay to better shape the wings of the nostrils. These will stay open and enable you to breathe through the finished mask.

11. You need not finish the clay mold in one day but never allow it to become dry. If you should need to leave it for any length of time, be sure to cover it with a wet cloth. Also, leave extra clay in the plastic container to keep it moist.

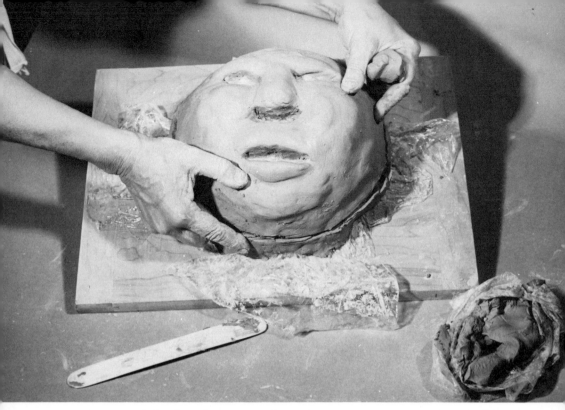

Features defined with eye, mouth, and nostril openings lifted out. Clay is added bit by bit to build up nose, mouth, cheeks and eye sockets.

Facial contour is redefined with edge of tongue depressor tool pressing onto bowl.

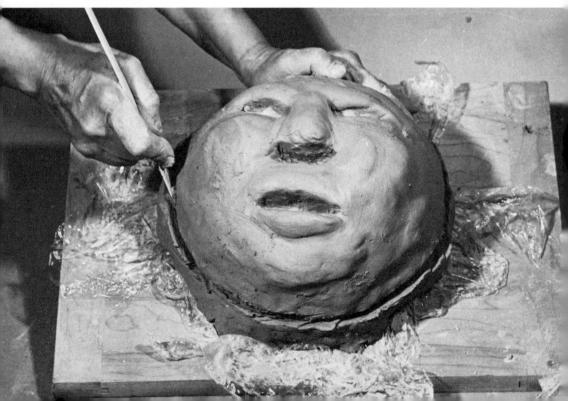

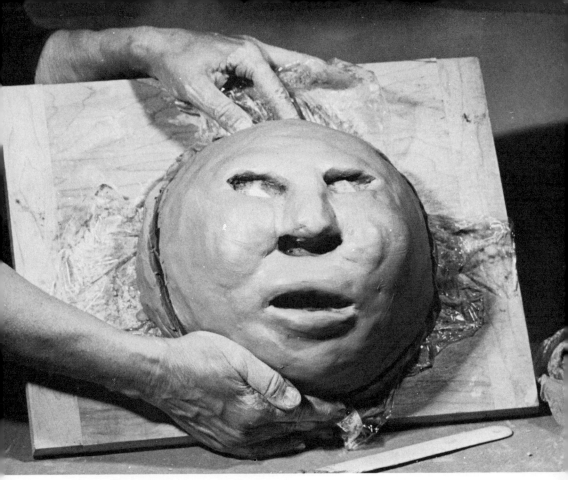

Finished clay mold with smooth surface.

12. When you are satisfied with your clay mold, wet your hand and smooth the rough surfaces to eliminate the need for much sandpapering of the finished paper mask.

13. With the edge of the tongue depressor tool, outline the facial contour. Press the tool into the clay until you can feel it making contact with the bowl but do not separate it from the rest of the clay which overhangs the bowl. This will become the outer limits of your mask.

14. Set the finished clay mold in a warm dry place and allow to dry thoroughly for about 3 or 4 days.

Papering the Mask
Materials:
2 double sheets colored comic newspaper
2 double sheets black and white newspaper
large size brown grocery paper bag
Vaseline or cold cream
small brush—an old shaving brush will do
wooden tongue depressor or a spoon
small amount of Rex dry powder wallpaper paste, or any wall-
    paper paste, or library paste

Directions:
1. Tear the sheets of colored comic newspaper, black and white newspaper, and the brown paper bag vertically with the grain of the paper into strips about 1½ inches wide and 6 inches long. *Never* cut the paper with scissors because the cut edges will make ridges in the finished mask. Torn edges will blend together. This mask will have three different layers of paper which will make it strong enough to wear. Papier-mâché masks can be made entirely of newsprint paper, but experience has shown that alternating layers of newsprint and wrapping paper makes them more durable.
2. Soak the three different papers in separate containers filled with water for one day.
3. Apply a thin layer of Vaseline or cold cream over the whole surface of your clay mold, making sure to get into all the crevices. This will prevent the dried papier-mâché from sticking to the clay later when you remove it.
4. For the first layer, lay the strips of colored comic newspaper over the clay mold, one at a time, horizontally, from ear to ear. Place the strips of paper a little beyond the contour line which you marked on the clay with the tongue depressor tool.
5. Be sure to slightly overlap each strip and gently smooth with

98

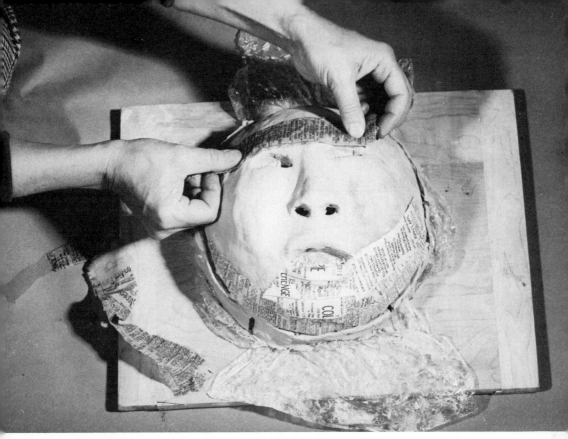

First layer of strips of newspaper applied horizontally to the mold.

your fingers to eliminate any air pockets under the paper. Use the brush for this reason too. Notice how the torn edges blend to maintain a working system. Start on one side of the face and proceed to the other side, without skipping around. Tear and use small pieces where necessary—under the nostrils, above and under the lips, around the corner of the eyes, around the wings of the nostrils, etc. Be sure that the paper goes over and beyond the contour of the clay and onto the board. Smooth out and stipple constantly with the brush where necessary. Pay particular attention to the corners of the eyes, nose, and mouth, and be sure to maintain the openings.

6. When the clay has been completely covered with strips of paper, tuck each overhanging end under the contour line of

the face all the way around. This will define the outer contour of the mask when the paper dries.

7. Prepare the paste. To do this, mix a small amount of powdered paste and water to a smooth, creamy consistency in a bowl. You may use library paste instead. Apply this over the papered mold with your fingers, much as one would apply cold cream to the face. Be sure to get into all the corners. When the paste is not in use, cover the bowl to prevent it from drying.

8. Remove the excess paste from the mask with your fingers. Do not allow any lumps to remain, no matter how small. These will make the finished mask bumpy.

9. For the second layer use strips of wet black and white newspaper. Lay these strips in a *vertical* position from hairline to chin, again slightly overlapping the edges of each strip. Apply and gently press the second layer with your fingers so as not to tear the first layer of paper. Follow the same procedure as for the first layer, until every bit of the first layer of paper has been covered.

10. For the third layer, repeat this procedure with the strips of brown grocery bag paper, this time *horizontally.*

11. Do *not* apply anymore paste, but allow the papier-mâché to dry in a warm, dry place for about two days. It is recommended that papering the mask be done in one sitting. Never allow the paper to become dry. If at any time it is necessary to leave the papering before finishing the work, cover it with a wet cloth.

A note of advice. Since skills are acquired through practice, you will improve with experience. Therefore, if you are not satisfied with the outcome of the mold or the papering, start over again.

12. When the papier-mâché is thoroughly dry, sandpaper any

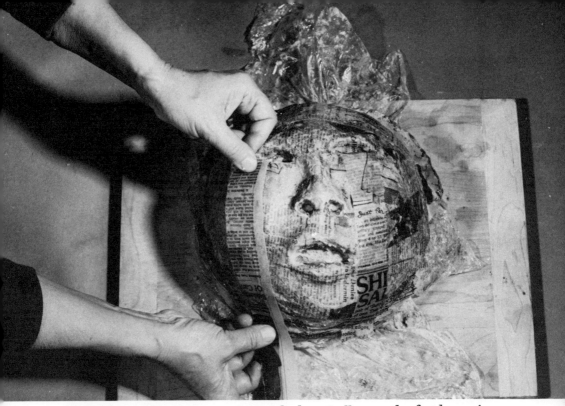

Second layer of newspaper strips applied vertically over the first layer of paper. Note how all corners of the features are covered with paper.

Third layer of strips of brown grocery bag paper are applied horizontally over the second layer of paper.

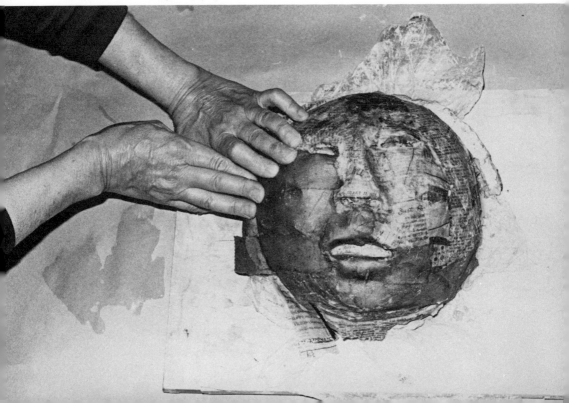

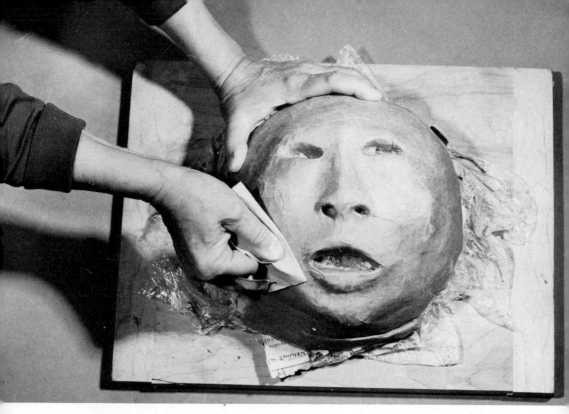

Mask is completely covered with third layer of strips of brown grocery bag paper. It is thoroughly dried and the surface is smoothed with a piece of fine sandpaper.

rough surface or paper edges with a piece of fine sandpaper. Brush off the paper dust.

13. Using the handle of a knife, gently tap and crack the clay rim. This is the part that extends over the contour of the mask and is resting on the base board. Remove the cracked pieces bit by bit. This will disengage the mask from the bowl.

14. Remove the mask from the bowl. Turn the mask with the inner clay side facing you and crack the clay with the handle of a knife. Remove the cracked pieces bit by bit till all of the clay has been removed from the papier-mâché. (See photo.)

If any repair work is necessary, now is the time to do it. Major repairs can be done by using strips of wet brown paper

Completed clay mold.

Inner clay mold is being broken with the handle of a knife a little at a time and the pieces of clay removed.

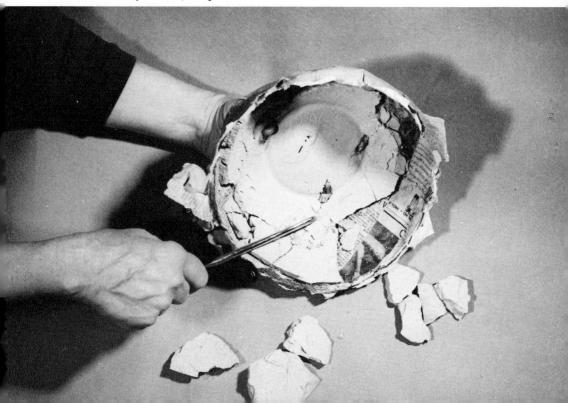

bag and paste. With minor repair work, use only the paste to fill small crevices. Allow to dry thoroughly.

15. Trim off any extending pieces of paper with a small curved cuticle scissors. Be very careful when cutting around the facial contours and near the eyes, nose, and mouth. If you are not careful, you may change the whole expression of the mask.

16. Wipe off any excess Vaseline from the inner surface.

17. Reinforce the contour edges of the mask with masking tape or gummed paper. Use two layers of tape to make a sturdy edging all around the mask.

Painting the Mask

Since the color of the Eskimo's skin tends to be brown, this particular mask can very well be used without painting because the surface layer of the paper bag has a rich brown color of its own. However, it is advisable to paint all papier-mâché masks to make them more durable. Paint will close the pores of the paper and make it stronger.

This mask can be painted with tempera or oil paints. Since masks become soiled with handling and wearing, oil paint is recommended because it is easier to clean with a moist cloth. Tempera, being water soluble, cannot be treated in this manner. Also, oil paint is more durable than tempera and will last longer without cracking. Another advantage of using oil paint is the shine it produces when it dries. When worn by an actor in motion, natural or artificial light will play on the shiny surface and give a life-like quality to the mask.

A general rule in painting a mask is to avoid monotony of color. It is suggested that at least two coats of paint be used. Make the first coat a dark brown and the second coat a lighter brown by adding more white to the basic color. Color combinations suggested here are only to guide those who are unfamiliar with oil painting. For our purpose, we shall use oil paints.

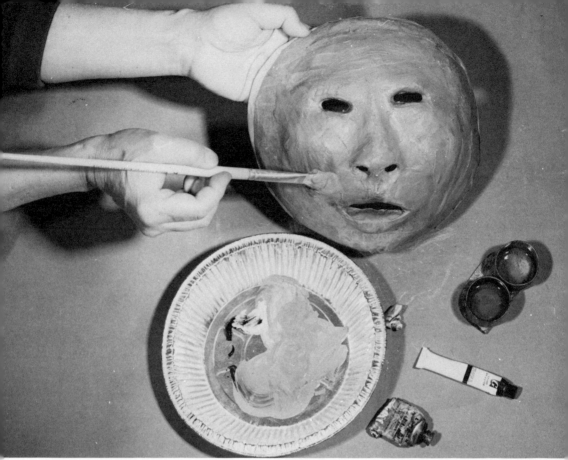

Papier-mâché mask is painted with oil paints.

Materials:

oil paints—Van Dyke Brown, Burnt Sienna, White

oil painting medium (small bottle of linseed oil and rectified turpentine)

small size paintbrush

small amount of turpentine for cleaning the brush

Directions:

1. For the first coat of paint, start with a mixture of white to which has been added a small amount of Van Dyke brown and Burnt Sienna. Squeeze a small amount of color from each

tube onto a wooden board (palette) or aluminum pie pan. Dip your brush into the painting medium kept in a small tin receptacle and mix the colors a little at a time. This will thin the paints as you go along, until you have mixed a shade of brown to your satisfaction. It is suggested that you keep this basic brown on the dark side. Apply this basic brown to the mask with the brush, making sure to cover all corners. If you wish, you may experiment by adding the three basic colors of red, blue, and yellow to white, instead of the ones mentioned. These colors, if used in correct proportions, will also result in a brown.

2. The second coat of paint should not solidly cover the first. Add more white to the basic brown color on your palette for the highlights such as the forehead. Add more Van Dyke brown and Burnt Sienna for the darker parts of the mask. Apply the second coat of paint loosely so that the darker brown underneath will show through in places. This technique of "overpainting" will simulate a more realistic coloring of the mask.

3. Allow to dry thoroughly.

4. To preserve the inner surface of the mask, paint it with a coat of clear lacquer, varnish, or oil paint. When hardened, it will prevent softening of the paper from perspiration and thus give additional strength to the mask.

5. Allow the mask to dry thoroughly before decorating.

Decorating the Mask With Simulated Fur

Materials:
cardboard approximately 13 inches by 3 inches
thick heavy Jiffy Knit yarn or heavy Christmas tie yarn (if yarn is not available, use strips of crepe paper or newspaper glued around the mask, one at a time)
scissors
masking tape
stapler

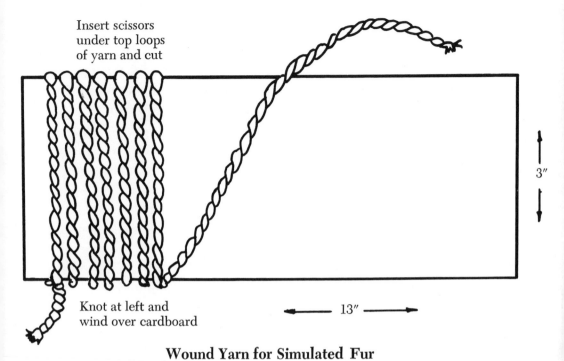

Insert scissors under top loops of yarn and cut

3"

Knot at left and wind over cardboard

13"

Wound Yarn for Simulated Fur

Directions:

1. Hold the cardboard with the long side at the bottom. Starting at the left side, wind the yarn once around the 3 inch width and tie with a knot to hold. Continue to wind the yarn around the cardboard (see sketch) progressing from left to right. When the end of the cardboard has been reached, cut the yarn off the skein.

2. Lay the yarned cardboard flat on the table. Apply the upper half of a strip of masking tape at the bottom of the full length of the yarned cardboard. Press the tape firmly over the base of the looped yarn. Turn the yarned cardboard over and complete taping the reverse side with the other half of the masking tape. Press firmly to hold. Now the base of the looped yarn is held together with masking tape. To strengthen the connection, superimpose another piece of masking tape over the first one.

107

3. With the yarn still looped over the cardboard, cut the top loops of yarn by working the scissors under the looped edge. Remove the cardboard. Now you have a simulated piece of parka fur which will cover approximately one half of the mask.

4. Repeat this process for the second half of the parka fur.

5. For hair, use short pieces of yarn. Apply glue to each piece and attach it to the forehead of the mask. Press to hold. Allow to dry.

6. Place a strip of the simulated parka fur with the masking tape flat against the contour on the outer side of the mask. Staple this to the mask all the way. Repeat the process with the second half, till the simulated parka fur is attached all around the contour of the full mask. The top of the parka should fall just above the hairline, the sides just beyond the cheeks, and down around the chin.

7. To make the wool look more like fur, gently unravel each strand of yarn with your fingers, taking care not to pull it away from the masking tape. This is a tedious task but well worth the effort.

8. To prevent any scratching from the staples on the inner side of the mask, cover the inner contour with masking tape.

9. To attach the mask to your face, see the directions under *Some Things To Consider in Mask-Making*, step number 14, page 37.

10. Now your Eskimo mask is ready to be worn to the North Pole.

Epilogue

What can mask and pantomime entertainment mean to us today? Many of us know the enjoyment of wearing a mask, but an entirely new experience awaits those who wear masks of their own creation and write their own plays and stories. And pantomiming adds a new dimension because it is a subtle art which requires great imagination and concentration. It allows both the pantomimist and the spectator to escape from a world of realism and enter into a world of imaginative character interpretation. It is a form of entertainment that has humor and dignity and makes use of the finest creative effort.

More and more we read about performances with mask and mime being given not only by amateurs in schools but also by professionals on the legitimate stage. This in itself is an indication that masks and pantomime have once again come into their own and have a promising future.

Source and Reading List

The American Heritage Book of the Revolution. New York, American Heritage Publishing Co., 1958.

Baranski, Matthew, *Mask Making.* Worcester, Mass., Davis Publications, Inc., 1954.

Benda, Wladyslaw T., *Masks.* New York, Guptil Publications, Inc., 1944.

Columbia Encyclopedia, Third Edition. New York, Columbia University Press, 1963.

d'Aulaire, Ingri and Edgar, *Pocahontas.* Garden City, New York, Doubleday & Company, Inc., 1946.

Encyclopedia Britannica, Volume 15. Chicago, Encyclopedia Britannica, Inc., 1951.

Hobbs, William Herbert, *Peary.* New York, The Macmillan Company, 1936.

Hunt, Douglas and Kari, *Pantomine: The Silent Theatre.* New York, Atheneum Publishers, 1964.

Hunt, Kari and Carlson, Bernice, *Masks and Mask Makers.* Nashville, Tennessee, Abingdon Press, 1961.

Mills, Winifred and Dunn, Louise, *Marionettes, Masks, and Shadows.* New York, Doubleday, Doran & Company, 1927.

Petry, Ann, *Harriet Tubman.* New York, Thomas Y. Crowell Company, Inc., 1955.

Slade, Richard, *Masks and How to Make Them.* London, Faber and Faber, Limited, 1964.

Index